DATE DUE

BECKETT AND BEHAN

BECKETT

AND

BEHAN

and a Theatre in Dublin

by

ALAN SIMPSON

ROUTLEDGE AND KEGAN PAUL
London

First published 1962
by Routledge & Kegan Paul Ltd
Broadway House, 68–74 Carter Lane
London, E.C.4

Printed in Great Britain
by Latimer, Trend & Co Ltd, Plymouth

TO CAROLYN SWIFT
and all those who have worked for
and in the Pike Theatre, Dublin

CONTENTS

ILLUSTRATIONS

~~~~~~

INTRODUCTION

I AM NOT EQUIPPED—nor have I tried—to make this
book either a scholarly analysis of the works of
Samuel Beckett and Brendan Behan or a complete
and accurate pair of biographies. I have done very
little research and have just set down what I know,
believe and think about the two playwrights, the
Ireland from which they spring and the theatre of
the fifties in general.

My own somewhat unusual background and experience of Irish affairs and the theatre has placed me
in an almost unique position to comment on the
peculiar situation of the Irish playwright. I have therefore unashamedly digressed into matters which at
first glance may not seem to be strictly relevant to
my two subjects. I believe, however, that they will
give the reader a general background which should
serve as a basis for future study of the playwrights as
Irishmen and increase his appreciation of their plays.

I leave it to others—in the case of Beckett, Dr. A. J.
Leventhal would be the obvious man—to write
proper biographies in due course.

For the benefit of students and serious readers, I

give a list of the dates of various events mentioned in the text to compensate for my somewhat rambling style.

*   *   *

I wish to express my deep appreciation for the help given me in the writing of this book by Miss Seonaid Walker. I am also indebted to the under-mentioned for making available the illustrations:

Andrew Flynn, Esq.
Reginal Gray, Esq.
The Irish Press Ltd.
Derrick Michelson, Esq.
Michael Peto, Esq., of *The Observer*

CHRONOLOGY

1906 Samuel Beckett born in Dublin.

1916 Rising and Declaration of the Irish Republic at G.P.O. Dublin.

1921 The Author born in Dublin.

1922 Treaty between the Irish insurgents and the British Government setting up the Irish Free State.

1923 Brendan Behan born in Dublin.

1927 Samuel Beckett graduated from Trinity College, Dublin.

1937 Samuel Beckett settled in Paris.

1938 Beckett's first novel (*Murphy*) published in English by Routledge.

1939 Brendan Behan arrested in Liverpool in connection with I.R.A. activities.

1940 Samuel Beckett joins the French Resistance Movement.

1945 Samuel Beckett joins staff of Irish Red Cross Hospital at St. Lo.

1945 Brendan Behan, who had been interned as an I.R.A. man in Ireland (after his release from a British Borstal Institution and deportation) is released in Dublin.

1952 *En Attendant Godot* first performed in Paris at the Theatre de Babylone.

1953 Pike Theatre Club opened in Dublin.

1954 *The Quare Fellow* first performed at the Pike Theatre, Dublin.

1955 *Waiting for Godot* first performed in English in Arts Theatre, London, and Pike Theatre, Dublin.

1956 *The Quare Fellow* first performed at the Theatre Royal, Stratford, E. London.

1957 *Fin de Partie* (*Endgame*) first performed at Royal Court Theatre, London—in French.

1957 First Dublin Theatre Festival—'Rose Tattoo' case started.

1957 *An Goill* (*The Hostage*) first performed by Gael Linn in Damer Hall, Dublin.

1958 *The Hostage* first performed in the Theatre Royal, Stratford, E. London.

1958 *Borstal Boy* published.

1959 *Endgame* and *Krapps Last Tape* first performed in English at the Royal Court Theatre, London.

1959 *The Hostage* presented at Wyndham's Theatre, London.

1960 *The Hostage* presented at Cort Theatre, New York.

CHAPTER I

THE PIKE THEATRE, DUBLIN

WHEN, in September 1953, my wife and I were ready to open the small theatre we had been a year converting by our own part-time labour and that of three friends, our first task was to find it a name. It must be short, we decided realistically, because that would keep down newspaper advertising costs.

After much discussion, we fixed on 'The Pike', meaning the long pole with a spike on the end, which was used by the Irish insurgents of 1798 to discomfit the slick English cavalry. In other words, we wanted our theatre to be a revolutionary force of small means which, by its ingenuity, would stir up the theatrical lethargy of post-war Ireland.

Looking back on it today, we really didn't have any idea what we were doing and we only made this a sort of convenient excuse to ourselves for using the name. In fact, it now seems that we were in reality among the shock troops of a movement of change in the theatre, which was going on unknown to us throughout Europe.

We didn't make any vast claims for the organization we were setting up. In fact, all we said in the circular which we sent to potential members, was that we intended starting a theatre 'for the presentation of plays which, for one reason or another, would not otherwise be seen in Dublin'. In reply to the circular, we got a postcard from someone who said they had heard we were going to perform Samuel Beckett's *En Attendant Godot*. 'If this is the case', read the postcard, 'I will become a member of your theatre club.'

I had been professionally engaged in the theatre since 1945, when I had joined Hilton Edwards and Micheál MacLiammoir as stage manager, and I had mixed a lot with a literary and artistic bunch whom I now know (as police witnesses say in evidence) to have been what today are called 'Beatniks'. But I wasn't really a literary type and, for some reason Beckett's early novels hadn't penetrated my particular set.

However, I made a few inquiries and found out all about him, for those of Dublin's literary circles who were in touch with what was going on in Paris knew plenty about Beckett and this new play which was having such success in the tiny Babylone Theatre. I then met a French girl, working in the French Cultural Centre in Dublin, who was a great Beckett fan and anxious to translate *Godot*, so I wrote to the author in Paris, asking if he would consider letting her do it for production in the Pike. I got a nice letter back, saying that he had himself translated the play for publication in the U.S. and would send me a typescript of it as soon as it was ready and that I was very welcome to do it in Dublin. This was my initial connection with Samuel Beckett.

1(*a*). The Pike Theatre auditorium during construction.

1(*b*). A set on the twelve-foot square stage.

2. Herbert Lane outside the Pike.

Brendan Behan I had met in the beat group mentioned above shortly after he came out of internment in 1946, when I was working in the Gaiety Theatre with Hilton Edwards. Our first meeting was dramatic. Brendan, though thinner in those days, appeared, to say the least of it, tough and, to people who didn't know him well, rather frightening. He happened to be in the studio that was our after-hours headquarters when I arrived in one of my rare, but violent tempers. My motor-bike had been stolen from outside the stage door, and I vented my rage on the furniture, throwing chairs and so on with such effect that Brendan—used as he was to the harsh ways of policemen and prison warders—was much intimidated. He treated me with great respect for some time after this and still refers to the incident when introducing me to his underworld friends!

At that time Brendan had, as far as I know, no thoughts of being a playwright. He had published some Irish language verse in an I.R.A. paper and the Gaelic monthly *Compar*, and subsequently had a short story called *A Woman of No Importance* published in *Envoy*, a magazine run by my friend (and subsequent partner) John Ryan. But Brendan was interested, as most of us were at that time, purely in drinking, politics and parties.

I broke with this light-hearted existence when the financial demands of marriage and prospective fatherhood forced me into the traditional Irish remedy of emigration. I spent a year in England, working first with an architect and subsequently in a Bermondsey building contractor's office, but then returned to Dublin to rejoin the Irish Army, which I had left in

1945 to become stage manager at the Gate. I secretly hoped to be able to combine my military duties with occasional theatrical productions for one or the other of the Dublin managements, for I had wanted to produce ever since my student days, and this desire had been stimulated intensely by working under Hilton Edwards.

But in the Dublin of the late forties and early fifties, there was not much opportunity for the free-lance producer. The Abbey had been, for many years, very much a closed shop in this respect and not since the days of Hugh Hunt had they employed a producer who did not have a long previous association with the organization. Moreover, since Ernest Blythe gained full control, the Irish language had become an important factor in his selection of associates, whether actors or otherwise. This put me at a disadvantage for, while I quite approve of the efforts to revive the language, I was educated at Campbell College, Belfast, where to put it mildly, Irish was not an approved subject on the curriculum. Since leaving school, I had been too occupied with other matters and hadn't sufficient real enthusiasm or gifts to get down to learning it.

On the other hand, the Dublin Gate Theatre had its own producer in Hilton Edwards. Hilton had dominated the Irish theatre, outside of the Abbey, since 1928, when he and Micheál MacLiammoir had founded the Gate and had brought all the more exciting dramatists of Europe and America to the Dublin stage. During the war, due to the impossibility of obtaining English touring companies he had filled the resultant gap in the Gaiety Theatre bookings and, by the time I joined him, was definitely in what would now be called the Establishment Class. He fought bravely against the pressing need for popular success to fill a large theatre, but was forced by economic pressure to perform mostly plays deemed by the Gaiety management likely to prove good box-office, although this did not prevent some wonderful Shakespearian productions, as well as Wilde and Shaw. So, in 1951, becoming restive under the routine duties of peace-time military life, I determined that the only thing to do was to start a company of my own.

Hilton and Micheál had shown that the only way to build up an individual theatrical organization was to have a theatre building at your disposal—the story of those years has been well told by MacLiammoir in *All for Hecuba*—but the economic situation, both in the theatre and outside it, had radically changed since the pre-war days of cheap labour. The average prices of theatre seats in Dublin—and indeed, elsewhere— had not risen greatly, whereas the costs had risen tenfold. Therefore, the acquisition of a building even as well appointed as the Gate, or its tiny forerunner, the hundred-seater Peacock Theatre, where the Gate had its first shows, was out of the question.

Some Paris mini-theatres and a couple of tiny art theatres in Dublin—the '37' and the 'Studio', which had been running in Georgian basements—gave me inspiration. After a long search, we found a premises which, though not suitable, was just possible—just within our means. Apart from the difficulty of a comparative new-comer getting backing for a large project, there is something to be said for keeping well within your means. By having such a tiny theatre, we were able to put a higher proportion of investment into each show than would have been possible had we been working on a larger and more 'economic' scale. My job in the army meant that I was not too worried by the actual problem of living, and we devised a co-operative system whereby our profits from each show were divided equally between the Equity members of the cast, of which I counted as one. Our minute size meant that costs, such as paint, canvas, etc., were kept to the minimum and the Front of House was staffed by press-ganged friends and would-be actors. Thus we had a free hand in our choice of play, our only limitation being the actual size of the stage, which was twelve feet by twelve feet. This had the sad effect of preventing us from giving the first performance in English of Ionesco's *The Chairs*. We simply did not have room on the stage for the chairs themselves.

For the size of the theatre, I was able to have, comparatively speaking, much more lighting equipment than would be possible in a larger building and, by its use, minimized the difficulties caused by the close proximity of the audience to the stage and the smallness of the stage itself. I used a method of lighting which I had learnt from watching ballet: this was to light from directly overhead and from the side, only using sufficient front lighting to heighten slightly the amount of light on the actors' faces. All the lighting I used was directional: that is to say, there was no spilling or flooding of light over the stage and, by this method, I achieved a three-dimensional emphasis on the actors which made the stage look bigger than it really was. Had we not had our own premises, however, this would hardly have been possible, since a landlord might not have understood the absolute necessity of cutting out the floor of the room above to permit a proper throw of light!

I have used this lighting technique—and I have seen others use it—in larger theatres, and it is certainly worth the attempt if it can be brought off. It is very difficult, however, because the distance to the back seats in a big theatre means that there must be a lot more light on the actors' faces if their expressions are to be properly seen. To achieve this, it is necessary to know your lights, colours and switchboard thoroughly, a very difficult job in a large theatre, where there may be hundreds of different lights and thousands of different combinations and permutations in their placing. But in the Pike, with about twenty lights to play around with on a space no bigger than the average No. 1 dressing-room, I had the opportunity of getting the very most in the way of depth and solidity.

In other words, I achieved something in the nature of a 3-D theatre, making the audience feel they were a part of the play and involving them in its action and atmosphere. This question of atmosphere seems to me to be all-important. Once you can establish the atmosphere, everything else follows. But it does lead to extremes in audience reaction, since no one can sit outside the play and enjoy or criticize it on a purely intellectual basis. They are emotionally involved and 'feel', rather than think, that the play is 'wonderful', or 'disgusting', 'deeply moving' or 'degrading'.

This is borne out by the back-handed tributes of several 'old-lag' friends of Brendan's, who declared that they really felt they were 'inside' again while watching *The Quare Fellow*.

I think, too, that it explains the extraordinary episode of *The Rose Tattoo*, which I shall be dealing with in a later chapter, when four ordinary Irish plain-clothes-men, who had little or no experience of theatre-going, suddenly found themselves plunged almost literally into a sun-baked tin-roofed house in the Southern States and involved in Latin emotion and love-making which was so far outside their normal experience as to create in them feelings of violent embarrassment.

I have found, from working in the Pike, that my only true satisfaction in theatre comes from the creation of a complete involvement of emotion, whether it be happy or sad, between audience and cast. This can happen occasionally in the cinema, with such films as *La Strada* and *Porte des Lilas*, but it is rare. In Dublin, it can be a stimulating experience for producer or manager to stand at the back of his theatre, feeling the waves of his audience's emotion moving about him. In London, one gets the feeling that the audience, having had a good dinner, have marched themselves to their seats, made themselves comfortable and then said: 'Right, now entertain us!'

A further example of reaction in the Pike, was during performances of Sartre's unpleasant play, *Men Without Shadows*, when we regularly used to have to bring out female members of the audience in a fainting condition to the lane outside, where they were

8

draped across the bonnets of parked cars, for lack of any better means of dealing with them, sometimes as many as three cars being pressed into service at the one time!

The play deals with the capture and torture by Vichy police of members of the Resistance, and one of the characters is a sixteen-year-old boy. This was, in fact, played by a sixteen-year-old schoolboy who, though good, had not the serious Devotion to Sincerity which I usually expect from my cast. During the scene in which he is strangled by one of the other prisoners to prevent his talking under torture, his position was such that the audience could see the face of his strangler without being able to see his. The actor playing the strangler was giving of his emotional best to such effect that a woman in the front row, only three feet from where the boy was in his death throes, gasped: 'Oh, no! No!', whereupon the wicked boy winked at his murderer, who was forced to conceal his suppressed giggles by grimaces of horror and determination!

But perhaps atmosphere is most important of all in the works of Tennessee Williams. I have never been in the Southern States of the U.S., but I feel that Tennessee Williams is to them as Pinter in *The Caretaker* is to suburban London: that is to say, he distills the atmosphere from a certain decayed stratum of the area about which he is writing, and I think *atmosphere* is the whole key to presenting Tennessee Williams on the stage. Perhaps I can understand this atmosphere particularly well, because there is much in common between the twilight world of Tennessee Williams in the Southern States, and mouldering

9

Anglo-Ireland. Both are peopled with shabbily-genteel, frustrated spinsters, harassed and inept clergy, and the rotting aristocracy, ineffectually trying to ignore the changing times and drawing their sole comfort from reminiscence about the real or imaginary glories of the past.

My father, like Tennessee Williams's, was a clergyman, and a clergyman, moreover, working, in the latter part of his life, among a kindly, respectable but completely left behind and useless collection of what my wife and I used unkindly to call 'Zombies'.

Human beings, no matter what their background, have to cling to some real or imaginary 'set', in order to preserve that precious commodity—self-respect. In *The Caretaker*, right to the end of the play, Pinter's tramp preserves the myth that he is going somewhere, and doing something—that he 'belongs'. In *Summer and Smoke*, Alma Weinmiller clings to her imagined love affair with the feckless young doctor. In *The Glass Menagerie*, the mother clings to her delusions that her daughter is attractive and marriageable, and that they are living in a world of Grand Balls and a complex of social commitments. So it is that the elderly Church of Ireland ladies clutter the mantelpieces of their shabby bed-sitting-rooms with pictures of the Dear Queen, wedged precariously between faded photographs of a nephew killed on the Somme and souvenir portraits of Lord Roberts.

While Tennessee Williams seems to be noted mainly among the public at large for his dramatic expositions of the weirder side of sex, I think it is much more essential for his plays that a producer

should succeed in establishing real contact with these
dear deluded people than that he should create any
coup de théâtre with the more melodramatic side of his
plays.

So, in fact, I see Tennessee Williams, Arthur Miller,
Samuel Beckett, Pinter and Ionesco, all apparently
dealing with completely different facets of life, but
all in fact revealing their compassion for the human
need to 'belong'. With Pinter and Tennessee Williams working on a more-or-less realistic plane, you
have the unbalanced mind, with its delusions of
activity and importance, used as an allegory to
demonstrate the author's pity for mankind. Beckett
and Ionesco, on the other hand, do not need the
device of mental derangement or eccentricity to
bridge the gap between delusion and imagined
reality.

Ionesco, perhaps, is less sympathetic than the others,
but he does reveal a similar insight into human self-
delusion, particularly in *The Chairs*. In the case of
Beckett—dealt with more fully in later chapters—the
two tramps are kept going solely because they are
waiting for Godot, even though they know that
Godot will never come; just as the old couple in *The
Chairs* usher in their mythical guests; the heroine of
The Glass Menagerie waits for her gentleman caller;
Willie Loman for his ship to come in, and Pinter's
tramp for his papers. And for that matter, the trivia
of surburban life with which the married couple in
Ionesco's *The Bald Prima Donna* surround themselves
are as much a form of escapism as the social fantasies
of the mother in *The Glass Menagerie* or the love life
of Alma Weinmiller. In fact, in real life, are the self-

important, jet-propelled flittings from capital to capital of the international business tycoon, of any more actual importance to the cosmos than the imaginary errands of an eccentric old Protestant lady in a shabby Dublin suburb?

This is a question that would never have been asked by a playwright of the post 1914–1918 War period. At that time, the Western world thought everything could be settled by this plan or that policy. Perhaps it is a measure of the disillusionment of the Second World War and, at the same time, one of the few good things to emerge from it, that thinking people (amongst whom, thank God, at least some playwrights can be included) now realize the importance of the individual sufficiently to ask such a question.

Nevertheless, when we started the Pike in 1953, we had no very strong ideas on the sort of plays we wanted to do. Tennessee Williams first began to interest me particularly about that time. During our first production (a hitherto unperformed work of Chesterton's, which we regarded as 'safe' and cultural—and which was a considerable flop) I met an American negro architect, who was visiting Dublin and who told me about *Summer and Smoke*. He promised to send me a script from New York. He was one of the few people I ever met under such circumstances who kept such a promise.

I read *Summer and Smoke*, which had been performed with only moderate success in London a couple of years previously. We had run a late-night revue that Christmas which had had great success and popularized our tiny theatre, and I felt we should follow up with something a bit more exciting than the two plays which had preceded it. *Summer and Smoke* was a very difficult play from a staging point of view, involving as it does a clergyman's study, a doctor's consulting-room and a public park, all simultaneously in view of the audience—somewhat alarming demand for a twelve by twelve stage. But my determination to ignore the difficulties paid off, and the experience gained from this production taught me that nothing is theatrically too difficult if you put your mind to it.

Another author with whose work I became familiar then was the Italian, Ugo Betti. I was in Paris on a short holiday with my wife immediately before the Pike opened—the last holiday I was to have for many years. We went to an exhibition of theatrical drawings and fell into conversation with the artist, who told us, after having heard of our project for a *théâtre de poche* in Dublin, that we must go to a theatre called 'Les Noctambules' (now, sadly, a cinema) to see a French tanslation of Betti's *Ile des Chèvres*. We were both deeply impressed by this production, which we saw, in fact, only at the second attempt. It turned out that there were two little theatres in the same lane and we had at first gone to the wrong one, spending a rather dreary evening watching a production by Finnish students of two Finnish plays in Finnish. One was rather intense, sad and Nordic-Slav; the other some sort of frolic about woodsmen in a woodsmen's hostel, involving a lot of horseplay and the removal—for frivolous reasons quite unconnected with sex—of one another's trousers! However, undeterred, we returned the following night to the right theatre.

13

For four years I chased from agent to impressario and back again in an attempt to get the rights of this play, which perhaps shows those people who say to someone running a theatre: 'Why don't you do some of So-and-so's plays?' how difficult it frequently is to line up an interesting programme. In fact, Denis Johnston once remarked to me that the main function of an agent would seem to be to *prevent* the production of plays in theatres. Let it be said, however, that some of my best friends are agents!

I finally produced *Ile des Chèvres* in 1958. It is a difficult play, not this time for staging reasons (as it has one simple set and a cast of only five) but in order to convey fully the emotional and claustrophobic atmosphere. When carefully cast, which I'm given to understand it was *not* in the States, it can be a very moving experience. It is about a con man of vague middle-European background, who battens on and sleeps with the widow of a university professor, her daughter and her sister-in-law, and is subsequently murdered by the mother. It makes considerable sense, if read in conjunction with some of the works of Simone de Beauvoir. In a way, it is comparable to plays of Sartre, such as *Huis Clos*, and the works of the other Italian, Diego Fabbri, who might be described as a Catholic Sartre, and with whose play *Inquisition* we had great success at the 1959 Dublin Theatre Festival.

I find it difficult to put these plays into any sort of category, except to call them plays of emotion, dealing with the relationship between men and women. Eugene O'Neill is probably the dramatic father of them all. Anouilh, whose plays I have never produced, I do not include in this group because he seems to me to lack the compassion for his characters which is held by Brendan Behan, Samuel Beckett, Jean Genêt and O'Casey, as well as those I have just mentioned. This compassion seems to be, so far as I can judge, the only connecting link between all the plays I have found real satisfaction in producing.

One great disadvantage of running a theatre in Ireland is that, while our closest neighbour is England, we have much more in common theatrically with America and France. We feel strongly about things —perhaps sometimes a little foolishly—but every member of an Irish audience has a much greater emotional reaction to what he sees and hears on the stage than his English counterpart. Thus, it is very rare for a production which has been successful in Dublin to move with equal success to London. I believe that if it were not for the language barrier in the case of France, and the distance barrier in the case of the U.S., we should have much more chance of close theatrical liaison between Dublin, Paris and New York.

An Englishman likes everything cut and dried. He likes his funny plays to be funny and his tragic plays to be tragic. In Ireland, we see tragedy and comedy marching hand in hand, as in the works of O'Casey. In France and America, the same combination can be seen in Anouilh and the more serious works of Ionesco, on the one hand, and in Tennessee Williams on the other. Perhaps it is because of the English audience's objection to this mixture of comedy and tragedy that English productions of plays by these authors always tend to be unbalanced, stressing one aspect at the expense of the other. This tendency is already handicapping the new English playwrights, such as Pinter, Osborne and Delaney, who are beginning to follow the example of France, Ireland and the U.S. by combining comic and tragic elements in their plays, for such works rarely get an even production and the only certain thing is that the English audiences will undoubtedly laugh in the wrong places.

In Ireland, on the other hand, there is an ideal audience for this mixture, for they are very quick in their reactions. A good actor can play on his audience's emotions, making them laugh one minute and cry the next. Also, the Irish—outwardly at any rate —are a prudish race, and therefore it is easy to shock them. This again means that the dramatist, producer and actor can, without going too near the bone for decency, glue the audience to their seats with the merest hint of delicate matters.

The lack of this sensitivity in English audiences is very apparent to me from going to the theatre in London. It seems that the English broad-mindedness, tolerance and ability to laugh at themselves has gone so far that—short of presenting a copulating couple or shouting obscenities about the Royal Family— neither of which would be permitted by the good Lord Chamberlain—nothing would really move them nowadays.

Where Irish and French audiences differ is that the French are willing to listen to a flow of words purely for the sound and pattern of them. While Irish audiences are similar to the French in their emotional reactions they—in common with their English and American fellows—immediately get restive if the

16

dialogue is not crisp and, in some cases, almost mono-syllabic. I find, for instance, that even such brilliant writers as Sartre can, to ears used to the English langu-age, sound repetitive in the extreme and judicious pruning of their plays greatly increases their chance of success with English-speaking audiences.

This, I think, explains the comparative unpopularity in English-speaking countries of French writers like Claudel, where the emotional content of the plays often seems lost in a welter of words. It is probably because French is, in itself, a beautiful language, but also, I think, because the French are very precise in their ideas and philosophies and are prepared to listen in a theatre to the exposition of ideas alone. All English-speaking audiences, whether in Britain, Ire-land or the U.S., want action all the time. It was for this reason that I rejected a play by Ugo Betti, trans-lated under the title of *Scales of Justice*, because its entire action was in the ideas, ethical and philosophi-cal, that it expressed. *Ile des Chèvres*, although classed by a Dominican priest friend of mine as a play of ideas (and part of the struggle that had been going on in France between Catholic philosophy and existential-ism) was carried along for me—and for the audience—by its conflicts of emotion. One of the most terse plays I have ever read is Shelagh Delaney's *A Taste of Honey*, and yet—in production—the monosyllabic nature of the dialogue passes unnoticed in the intensity and poignancy of the emotions it reveals.

Some modern authors—Tennessee Williams in par-ticular—seem to deal almost entirely with one type of emotion: in his case, frustrated sexual desire. Irish authors, on the other hand, while their plays tend to be plays of emotion, do not seem able to cope with sex at all, frustrated or otherwise. Even the great O'Casey, though filled with a desire to drive out prudery from the Island of Saints and Scholars, seems unable to achieve anything but a cardboard model of sexual emotion, even when he is trying as hard as he is in *Cock-a-Doodle Dandy*.

The drama of the inter-war period seems in retrospect to have been exemplified by the comparatively emotionless expressionist play. I think myself that there is some link between the fact that the 1914–1918 War was to be 'the war to end all wars', and the ideas of the immediate post-war period which were equally cut and dried. The immediate manifestation of this in the theatre was the stylized, emotion-free expressionist play, as in the visual arts it was cubism and straight-line architecture. After the disillusionment of the 1939–1945 repetition, people seemed to realize their frailty as human beings, and architects now see that men cannot live in straight lines alone, but need decoration and colour in their buildings, while playwrights have come to realize the need to deal with delicate, intangible emotions, where heretofore they had been dealing with formal ideas, as exemplified by the plays of the Čapek brothers, or Ernst Toller.

Although he spans such a long period and his plays, of course, are not formalized in an Expressionist way Bernard Shaw really comes into this category. His plays all have a slightly antiseptic logical quality, which I think explains the decrease in their popularity today.

But undoubtedly the outstanding feature of the theatre of the fifties is the emergence of the new non-

3. Brendan Behan.

4. Behan with some of the cast of *The Quare Fellow*.

realistic drama. Beckett, followed by Ionesco and Adamov in Paris, now have eager converts in England in N. F. Simpson and Pinter. The plays of these authors are quite different from the expressionist drama of the twenties and thirties. Although they do not tell a story and, at times, perhaps have some links with Brecht's famous 'alienation effect' in that they achieve their 'alienation' in some cases by deliberately scoffing at theatrical convention, these are *emotional* plays and, again I think, are manifestations of the appalling disillusionment of a second world war and the realization that we are all individuals seeking for love and communication one with another. In the classical plays of O'Casey, you have a stream of emotional effects played one after another on the audience, but *arising out of a plot or story*. In the case of the new, non-realists, it is as though the author had sat down and listed a number of emotions to which he wished to subject his audience, and then collected a number of non-realistic situations to fit the emotions.

A play of Ionesco's which had its first English-language performance in the Pike was *Victimes du Devoir*. In this play, which I do not think is fully successful, it is very apparent that the author is trying to conjure up a series of emotions, ranging from terror to love, and including such unusual theatrical sensations as claustrophobia and dizziness. I was not entirely satisfied with my production of this play, partly due to casting difficulties, but I subsequently saw a French production which was, I felt, equally unsatisfactory, though in a different way.

I first heard of Ionesco as a writer through Sam

Beckett. As I couldn't afford to keep travelling to Paris, I had no means of knowing how I should like his work, although I naturally respected Beckett's judgement; and I was therefore delighted to see in *The Stage* that there was to be a reading of his play *The Bald Prima Donna* at the Institute of Contemporary Arts. I immediately wrote to Donald Watson, his English translator, for a copy of the play, and we gave it a production in 1956. This was the first staging of any of his plays in English.

Donald Watson is a remarkable translator. One of the big problems of the theatre today is that of translation, and much of the success of *Waiting for Godot* in English-speaking countries must be attributed to the fact that the author was able to translate himself. There seems no middle way between the translations of Christopher Fry and Nancy Mitford, who give their translations a personal flavour which insures their success in the English language but is a deviation from the French originals, on the one hand, and the academic and far too literal translations on the other. These latter invariably sound stilted, when spoken by the actors, and can do a great deal to ruin an otherwise exciting play, by giving it a combination of dullness and pretentiousness quite foreign to the original work. Donald Watson, however, seems so in tune with Ionesco and, at the same time, such a master of the English language, that he is able to reproduce flawlessly the French originals in English. One of the features of Ionesco's writing, particularly in *The Bald Prima Donna*, is his playing *on* words for meaning (puns) and *with* words for sound (a kind of humorous poetry). Watson does not attempt a literal translation of such lines, but substitutes exact English equivalents to the original French puns, or a combination of English words that give the same sound effect. His brilliance at this was brought home to me very strongly when I read an American translation of the play, which rendered the literal meanings of the words (even where they were chosen for sound or *double entendre* instead of meaning), making complete nonsense of a play which, at its best, runs the risk of seeming nonsensical to a prosaic audience.

Fortunately for us in the Pike, however, a feature of Dublin audiences is that they will take any new idea or unusual approach by an author or producer at its face value, and this was a great help in pioneering plays such as those of Ionesco. Dublin audiences are not constantly seeking to be 'in'—in fact, many of our social customs and behaviour patterns, even in urban Dublin, probably date back to pre-Christian times. There is a section of the population which has adopted English ways of doing things but, where fashions, theatre, architecture or any other cultural activity is concerned, most of us tend to be a little bit half-hearted and many years behind the crazes of our neighbours. This is apparent from Dublin architecture, which lagged anything up to fifty years behind Britain in the nineteenth century and, when London was plunging into Betjeman's *Victoriana*, Dublin builders were still happily erecting 'Georgian' houses. The effect of this slowness to get on cultural band waggons is that, when one does come out with something quite new and revolutionary, it is judged on its merits rather than whether it is 'in' or 'out'. Theatre managers and producers in England and

America are constantly to be found striving to present something that is new in the 'in' way!

That is not to say that the way of the theatre is not economically hard in Dublin. I was only able to afford the inevitable losses of an experimental theatre by serving as an Engineers Officer in the army from 8.45 a.m. to 4.30 p.m. and working in my theatre from 5 p.m. to 1 a.m., giving my already-overworked wife all the jobs which had to be done during 'military duty' hours, and it was not until comparatively recently that we were able to realize a financial success.

Nor have we been alone in our financial problems. The Abbey, despite the subsidy of a national theatre, has been forced to produce, year after year, a certain type of Irish commercially successful play. The Gate, which passed into the sole control of the late Earl of Longford a couple of years ago, when the city council demanded its rebuilding for reasons of public safety, proved too much of a financial burden even for his ample purse, and he was obliged to let it to anybody who could afford to pay. The two large theatres, the Gaiety and the Olympia, confine themselves of necessity to entertainment which their managers consider likely to prove highly popular, but their judgement in these matters is not always as strong as their financial needs and they have both had rather erratic passages during the last few years. In addition, there was a company started about the same time as the Pike, called the Globe theatre, which was run by a group of actors headed by Godfrey Quigley and Norman Rodway. Unfortunately, the only suitable 'home' they could find was the demonstration theatre

of the Gas Company in Dun Laoghaire, a seaside
suburb of Dublin. This meant that they had to produce a stream of suburban plays for their Dun Laoghaire audiences, although these have proved less
suburban in taste than their English counterparts. The
Globe also, as a management, made occasional forays
into the big theatres, with varying degrees of success,
but economic pressures forced the company into dis-
bandment. This is a definite loss to the Dublin theatre,
but their place has been taken by a company founded
about three years ago by Phyllis Ryan (Orion Productions) which continues the policy of presenting
well-produced plays in Dublin and Dun Laoghaire.

The Abbey is nowadays the constant whipping boy
of the Irish Theatre. A lot of the criticism levelled at it
from various quarters is often frivolous and unfair,
bearing in mind the peculiar circumstances under
which it has to work. The Managing Director,
Ernest Blythe, is a forceful personality and completely
thick-skinned where criticism is concerned. He has,
however, continued to run the theatre and to obtain
large sums of money from the Government, where a
lesser man might, under similar conditions, have
allowed the whole organization to collapse and disintegrate about him.

The most unhappy event to affect its recent for-
tunes was the burning down of the original theatre in
1951. With tremendous courage and 'show must go
on' spirit, the company played uninterruptedly, first
in the tiny hundred-seater annexe, the Peacock, and
then in the well-equipped but remotely situated
amateur theatre attached to the Guinness Brewery.
Then, with Government aid, the company moved to

a large cine-variety music-hall, called the Queen's Theatre.

The large size and uneconomic layout of this theatre (together with the fact that the directors felt it their duty to keep on both the Queen's staff and the loyal band of Abbey ushers, clerks and stagehands, who would otherwise have been out of employment) has made it absolutely necessary for the choice of plays presented in the Queen's to fit the lowest common denominator of Irish taste; and while I have earlier praised some aspects of Irish audience reaction, there is no doubt that the stage Irishman has his strongest supporters among many of his fellow-countrymen. In fact, if an actor has a tendency to overplay, to work in the present Abbey company seems completely to disintegrate his artistic integrity in this respect.

For reasons best known to himself, Mr. Blythe refused all offers of private assistance from America and elsewhere at the time of the fire, and has obtained all the money he requires from the State. Perhaps, as an ex-politician, he feels more competent to deal with the vagaries of governmental benefactors than with the strings that might be attached to rebuilding under private patronage. However, whatever his reasons, the net result has been a long delay, while the necessary funds are being worked through Parliament and, at the time of writing, the demolition of the old theatre has only just been completed.

Since I may have seemed to praise the Irish audiences unduly in comparison with their English neighbours, I feel I should equally stress the reverse side of the coin. The adoration of the stage Irishman, mentioned à propos of the Abbey, is undoubtedly the facet of Irish audience-reaction most undermining to serious theatre.

Conversation has always been a popular pastime amongst all sections of the Irish population, and the surprising lengths to which many will go purely in order to bring off a gag probably explains the phenomenon of the stage Irishman. This aspect of Irish wit has been stressed by nearly all writers dealing with the Irish scene, from Sommerville and Ross onwards, and it is as prevalent today as it ever was. I remember a few years ago, joining a crowd at the bottom of Grafton Street on a frosty morning, where a horse had slipped and was being unharnessed by its driver. A passer-by asked one of the bystanders what was going on and he replied, without a second's hesitation: 'Ah, sure they're only putting the cart before the horse!'

This gives a clue as to why we produce a high proportion of actors per head of the small population, for there is a natural aptitude for acting in nearly all of us. You often hear a story told in a pub by someone who has never been inside a theatre in his life, narrated with such dramatic effect as would have taken a foreigner years of training and experience in the theatre to achieve. However, natural aptitude is a two-edged weapon where the Irish Theatre is concerned, for—since the Irish theatrical renaissance, brought about by the Abbey and the Gate in the early part of this century—every man, woman and child in Ireland considers him or herself to be a budding Micheál MacLiammoir or Siobhan McKenna, without any further effort in the way of preparation for a theatrical career.

There is a great profusion of amateur dramatic societies throughout the country, many with remarkably high standards, and there are very few professional actors who have not come into the theatre through the amateur movement. This, however, has also led to a neglect of basic training: few Irish actors can sing properly, or perform any of the minor athletic accomplishments like fencing, simple dancing or acrobatics, which are part and parcel of the training of their foreign colleagues, and I think there is only one professional actor in Dublin who has had a ballet training.

This lack of painstaking preparation for professional life—and, indeed, for individual presentations —is very apparent in the theatre in Ireland. Productions and performances alike tend either to be so inspired as to blind one to their faults, or to be downright incompetent. Competence, in fact, is at a premium in nearly every branch of the theatre and this is not helped by the way Irish audiences so often spoil an actor with exaggerated enthusiasm. The exuberant hilarity which frequently greets some comic extravagance in Dublin can often blind both actor and foreign visitor, surrounded as he is by uncritical goodwill, to the severe limitations of an artist, and I have seen an actor, regarded in Dublin as the funniest thing since Chaplin, collapse like a pricked balloon under the cold critical appraisal of a London first night audience.

In the days when there were many Irish regiments in the British Army, they were most frequently used in the attack, where great dash and verve were called for, but were found indifferent material where it was

26

necessary to hold a position for any length of time, requiring painstaking and serious devotion to duty. I think that this aspect of the Irish character runs right through Irish life and can be seen clearly in our contribution to the theatre. If everything is going well in a theatrical company, morale will be excellent and fantastic heights of artistic brilliance will be reached but, if houses are half-empty and the show not voted 'the success of the year', the company's spirit will collapse and their performances deteriorate from night to night. The actors will blame one another, the management, the author, or any other convenient scapegoat for the lack of success they feel they deserve. An actor who is perfectly happy to play for a salary of £X if business is booming will, most illogically, start an enormous agitation for £X plus 10 if the house is nearly empty.

I think that, as a nation, we are very sensitive to atmosphere, which probably explains why an Irish village lay-about can, if transported to Boston or Birmingham, swing to the other extreme and become the live wire of local business or political life.

Most of what I have said about actors in this connexion, applies equally to the plays we produce: snatches of brilliance, clumsily tied together with an inadequate, rambling plot and no construction whatsoever. This is true even of O'Casey. But despite these shortcomings, Irish writers, whether of prose, poetry, or plays, seem to find their way regularly into the vanguard of world literature and dramaturgy.

At the present time, the best drama seems to be divided between the abstract yet entertaining intellectual exercise and the dynamic working-class 'slice of

27

life'. In their way, Beckett and Behan have opened up these two new roads for present and future playwrights.

Although Beckett did not pioneer the post war *drama of the individual* he symbolizes it in many minds. Behan's work, on the other hand, I believe to be a very strong contributory factor to the success in the English-speaking world of Miss Joan Littlewood and the more exuberant forms of *dramatized social realism*.

Just as French revolutionary thinking inspired the American revolution, which in fact predated the Fall of the Bastille in time, so *Waiting for Godot* stands relevant to Tennessee Williams and others who may have been writing before this Franco-Irish play burst upon an astonished world. Likewise, Brendan Behan's ebullient personality focused attention on a type of drama which undoubtedly would have been written and was in fact being written before he appeared drunk on British Television.

At the moment, western playwrighting seems to be going through what might be described as its 'sordid period'. All revolutions go through their blood baths —the pattern is repeated again and again: France, America, Russia, Ireland, Algeria, the Congo—the formula is always the same. As individuals working in the theatre we are powerless to change the pattern of events. We who produce and manage are merely the midwives at the birth of a new theatre. All we can do is to seek out and encourage any writing that is original and good, and put it before the public. It is the public who will ultimately decide what they want to see and how they wish to see it presented.

Chapter II

BRENDAN BEHAN

~~~~~~

I AM SURE that many people who meet Brendan Behan away from his Dublin surroundings regard him as some sort of unnatural phenomenon of Irish life, a prodigy owing little to his parentage and less to his early upbringing. Nothing could be further from the truth. To understand Brendan properly, it is essential to meet and get to know Stephen Francis Behan, his father.

Stephen is a roundy little man of some seventy-five years, about half Brendan's size but with a twinkle in his eye and a bouncy personality that makes itself felt in any company. He has an enormous zest for life and good fellowship, which is only diminished by the consumption of sufficient alcohol to render him literally comitose. From him, Brendan has inherited the robust and entertaining personality which has done so much to enhance his purely literary accomplishments. From his father also he has acquired the capacity for being at ease anywhere, from a French château to an East End of London fish and chip shop.

Behan senior, for instance, is thoroughly at home in John Ryan's Bailey Restaurant bar among an assortment of Oxford University rejects (immaculate in Dublin University ties), theatrical layabouts in orbit around international film stars, wealthy and well-oiled Dublin shopkeepers, and eminent and inebriated Irish poets and painters. He sits with assurance in the chair at executive meetings of the Irish National Housepainters' and Decorators' Trade Union, and is equally happy discussing the iniquitous penny increase on the pint with his neighbours, while fortifying himself at Flood's, the pub round the corner from 70 Kildare Road, Crumlin. This is the corporation house which has been the Behan's town residence since they were shifted by a benevolent municipality from the tenement in Russell Street where Brendan spent his early years.

Stephen has always operated on the simple basis of 'If you have it, spend it', first on necessities such as drink and then, if there is anything left over, on luxuries like food, clothing and shelter. He shows no observable *bourgeois* 'love' for his family of seven; he holds to no accepted code of behaviour except that of good fellowship, and yet, of all the fathers I could have had, were I to be given the choice, I personally would not wish a better than Stephen.

One of the problems that Brendan had to face when his literary earnings rocketed to an annual figure far greater than the combined incomes of his entire family and ancestry for many generations back, was the challenge of this simple philosophy. If, like Stephen, your drinking hours are restricted by the eagle eye of the foreman and the inexorable termination of your weekly pay packet on a Monday morning, together with the healthy penance of a daily climb at 8 a.m. to the top of an eighteen-foot ladder (property of R. G. Brady & Co., Painting Contractors) paint brush and pot in hand, your health will be enforceably safeguarded.

When Brendan discovered that, with a few hours hard work at a typewriter, he could transform the pearls of wisdom and wit that his father, in a similar vein, had been distributing free for fifty years to fifty different public bars in the city of Dublin, he found himself unable to adjust his new situation to the traditional Behan family code. The result was that he became ill and after a few false starts and alarums has now had to adopt the regnum of his former archenemies, the Pioneer Total Abstinence Association. It says a lot for his strength of character and inherited good humour that he can knock as much fun out of a glass of soda water as his companions can today from a half-dozen pints or a couple of balls of malt. Of all the heavy drinkers I have known who, at some stage of their career, have been forced by economic or medical pressures to adopt this drastic course he is the only one who has not become soured and embittered, or assumed a 'holier than thou' attitude towards his fellow-men. In the Army, woe betide the unfortunate officer, N.C.O. or soldier on trial before a man who has swapped the booze for the brass.[1]

If Brendan was fortunate in his choice of father, he was equally lucky with his mother, Kathleen. Kathleen comes from a remarkable and fabulous Dublin family. Her brother was Peadar Kearney, an Irish balladier and patriot who composed a vivid profusion of songs both humorous and patriotic, ranging from

[1] Since writing this chapter, it appears that Brendan has again fallen from grace. But of this more in Chapter VII.

'Courtin' in the Kitchen' to our stirring national anthem, 'The Soldier's Song'.

I have no doubt at all that Brendan can attribute some of his colourful phraseology to this connection; but, of course, the Behan family life is knit together by their enjoyment of singing. 'If there's money, there's drink; and if there's drink, there's song' might be said to be the family motto. This is of course true, to a lesser extent, of all Irish social occasions. It is as much of a social necessity to contribute a song to a party as it is for wedding guests to give a present in other countries.

The Irish theatrical tradition proper only started with the National Theatre in the early 1900's. In the past, the theatre had been the prerogative of the rich and, until the end of the nineteenth century, when the Irish *bourgeoisie* began to taste the fruits of the 'freedom' gained for them by Daniel O'Connell, the distinctions between the well-to-do Anglo-Irish gentry and the Irish people as a whole were as sharp as those between black and white in South Africa today.

This meant that the only art forms available were singing and story-telling, as they needed no costly equipment for their execution; and it also explains why the best Irish singing is unaccompanied. There is a vast selection of ballad melodies handed down from generation to generation. Nobody knows who was the original composer, and each new version twists the melody to suit a new set of words.

Kathleen's sister was married to P. J. Bourke, who was manager of the Queen's Theatre, then a lusty proletarian music-hall, now—temporarily—the Abbey Theatre. He also founded a theatrical costumiers which is carried on by his sons. The eldest son, Lorcan, is now the head of what practically amounts to an empire in Dublin's entertainment industry. Apart from the costumiers, the family operate a large ballroom, run the Dublin branch of the Strand Electric Stage Lighting Company, and various other enterprises. Lorcan's daughter, Grainne, is married to Eamonn Andrews, who, apart from his well-known visible television activities, is chairman of the new Irish Television service.

It was not until Brendan's explosion as an internationally famous writer, which was triggered off by his alcoholic television appearance in 1956, that the Behan side of the family were able to compete, on the material side of life at any rate, with their cousins. In fact, in the early days of Brendan's success story, before he had a dress suit custom-built round him, the Bourke's, in the interests of family solidarity, were only too delighted to supply him with evening wear ex stock, from that branch of the business.

Kathleen herself is a lovely person, and together she and Stephen form a living advertisement for marital bliss, without conceding a single point to 'middle-class morality' or respectability. There is no doubt that 70 Kildare Road is the untidiest and most neglected residence in the area, but I am convinced that it is also the happiest.

The whole family is steeped in the Socialist Republican tradition founded in Ireland by Wolfe Tone. After James Connolly's execution in 1916, the Labour and Separatist movements joined hands for a while and in February 1923, Stephen Behan found himself in Kilmainham Jail with his Republican comrades.

33

Kathleen had been married before, her first husband having been killed in the Republican cause, and she had two sons, Rory and Sean; but the first-born Behan, a lusty child to be called Brendan, came into the world while his father was 'inside'.

Under the rigours of the political situation, the prison regulations made it impossible for Kathleen to visit her husband to show him the new arrival, so secret arrangements were made for Stephen to be hoisted by his jail mates to a cell window at a certain time and Kathleen, below, would hold up the infant Brendan for his father to see.

Apart from half-brothers, Rory and Sean Furlong, there are three other Behan brothers and a sister. Carmel, the daughter, is married, and Seamus (the youngest) works as an electrician in London. It is Brian, the active organizer of the Socialist Labour League, and Dominic, the writer and balladier, who indicate that this is no ordinary family and that Brendan is no flash in the pan, as it were.

Brian is much quieter and more serious than the others, and has confined his activities strictly to the political field where he has remained rather a back-room boy. Apart from some headlines made when he was jailed in connection with the Shell Building strike, he has avoided the publicity which seems to surround all the rest of the Behans' activities. He is, in fact, a serious political philosopher in the Connolly tradition.

Dominic, on the other hand, has been dogged in his writing by his big brother's success, and a slightly neurotic tendency has magnified a natural rivalry between them. This was blown up and encouraged by

the Press, following an alcoholic incident just before
my production of Dominic's play, *Posterity be Damned*
in the Metropolitan Theatre, Edgeware Road,
London, in March 1960. It is to be hoped that the
years will mellow the two writer members of the
family, and that Dominic, who has a lot of successful
radio and television work to his credit, will come to
terms with the situation inherent in any family life,
but swollen out of normal proportions by the Press
interest in 'Behanry' in general.

After his family life, I.R.A. and prison experience ∠
(described vividly in *Borstal Boy*) the next important
influence on Brendan was the Bohemian life of
Dublin into which he plunged on his release from
internment in 1945.

Much has been talked and written about 'beatniks'
in the last few years. The 'beatnik' of the sixties seems
to me to be simply an individual (with origins in any
social or financial class) who has thrown over the
normally practised codes of social behaviour for his
particular background. In the Paris of the nineteenth
century they used to be called 'Bohemians'. In the
Dublin of the late forties and early fifties, it was the
'MacDaids crowd'.

Surely the 'beats' of today are just the artists,
writers and composers of the future, with their entourage of cultural layabouts. As the talent of the few
gains recognition over the years, the rest will go
respectable, die of malnutrition, or simply become
absorbed in some other way of life. Historians put
labels on periods: 'Restoration', 'Fin de Siècle',
'Edwardian', 'Post-war' and so forth, but the differences, though at times affected by such things as the

mass slaughter of 1914–18, are pretty superficial, and the unchanging cycle continues as generation succeeds generation.

The Dublin of the late forties and early fifties was affected materially by the physical proximity of a country which had been at war a few years previously. After years of isolation brought about by our neutrality in the war, we found ourselves an attractive centre of congregation for all sorts of foreigners. We did not have the food rationing and regimentation which still made it awkward for the young student Bohemian to go about his unlawful occasions in other countries. Many people who would, today or before the war, have gone to live in Paris, came to Dublin instead.

In the McDaids crowd, however, you had the slightly unusual ingredient of a dozen or so former I.R.A. adherents, recently released from long sentences imposed on them during the 1938–9 bomb incidents in Great Britain. The pub (McDaids) which was our main meeting-place is owned by a gentleman whom we used to refer to as 'Mr. Er'. This was because he could never remember the names of his clients, whom he addressed in this way, nor, for that matter, had he a clue what they were at or what they were talking about. Paddy O'Brien, the chief 'curate' integrated with us much more, and frequently came to the 'parties' which were the almost nightly sequel to 'Time, Gents, please!'

At first, these were held mostly in the studio of sculptor and papier-mâché artist, Desmond Mac-Namara, where I first met Brendan. Later, the epi-centre of our post-closing-time activities became the

'Catacombs', the Georgian basement flat about which Brendan is always threatening to write a play. The 'proprietor', a delightful but dissolute former London night-club official who is now manager of a smart cocktail bar in New York, was going through a very low period in his life. His only source of income was the sub-letting of various corners of the Catacombs for various purposes, and the sale of empties to a glass bottle merchant. This latter was his most regular and reliable means of support, as his tenants were quick to take advantage of his kind heart where the 'rent' was concerned. He occasionally did odd jobs of one sort or another, including acting as box-office manager for the first production under the Pike banner, which took place in Dun Laoghaire Town Hall. He was excellent at this work, except when some little windfall made it possible for him to ward off the municipal draughts with a bottle kept in the cash-box. Then he would indiscriminately address all potential ticket buyers as 'My Dear' and give them the treatment normally meted out to prospective clients at a Soho floor show.

While the genuine beatnik or Bohemian lives on the job, as it were, most of the MacDaids crowd were 'dayboys'. That is to say, we had homes, wives, parents, and other *bourgeois* accoutrements, to whom we returned at various hours of the day and night. I, of course, had the Army, and Brendan and Dominic numerous jobs with various firms of painting contractors. One of the more colourful figures in our circle was an American 'studying' at Trinity under the G.I. Bill of Rights, whom J. P. Donleavy took as his model for the *Ginger Man*, and in part, I suspect, for the central character in *Fairy Tales of New York*. Another 'day boy' was the aforementioned John Ryan, also an excellent painter, whose family owned a large Dublin business.

About this time, Ryan and Valentin Iremonger, the poet, now Counsellor of the Irish Embassy in London, started *Envoy*. Brendan, as he has described in *Borstal Boy*, had received a pretty good literary education at the various institutions where he had languished, and also from his father. But were it not for the contacts he made during this period, it might have been a very much longer time before his work gained general recognition—not merely the contacts in the material sense, but the effect of the example of others trying to express something new, through writing, painting or music, must have influenced Brendan. For surely, much as they are disapproved of in all orthodox societies, it is from these groups of 'social misfits' that the world's *avant-garde* writers, artists and musicians emerge, to become the accepted master of tomorrow.

As I mentioned before, Brendan's first publication in English was in *Envoy*. After various short contributions to a fairly wide assortment of newspapers and magazines in Ireland and a piece in a Franco-American literary magazine published in Paris, the big step was his employment by the Irish Press as a columnist. It was this that really enabled him to discard the paintbrush for the typewriter. The column was an instant success. Brendan's great gift is for anecdotage and colourful reportage—he is one of the most entertaining conversationalists I know. The world is fortunate that he has the ability to transfer scintillating and outrageous bar talk to paper.

Reading his newspaper articles and knowing the man, I was able to hear his voice in my mind's ear, and practically smell the bar smells that are so much a part of his way of life. About this time, he had written a radio script called *The Twisting of Another Rope*, which he had submitted first to Radio Eireann, and then, as a one-act play, to the Abbey. Whether on account of its gruesome subject (hanging), or because these Establishment bodies thought it was too nearly libellous of the prison warders and others connected with Dublin's major jail, I don't know, but at any rate it was rejected by both, though Mr. Blythe of the Abbey maintains that he suggested that the play might be accepted if rewritten. However, Brendan then blew it up into a three-act play and hawked it around the other large Dublin managements without success.

Since 1952, when my wife and I (together with Edmund Kelly, an army carpenter subsequently a co-director and resident stage manager) had started work on the construction of our theatre, I had been slightly less in contact with the MacDaids group. This was partly because there are only twenty-four hours in one day, and a full day's work in the Army, followed by an evening's navvying in the Pike, left little time for social contact; and partly because a friend tipped me off (with what authenticity I shall never know) that the Army Intelligence was taking an unfavourable interest in my frequent visits to the pub, which they regarded as a hotbed of all activities unsuitable to the spare time of an officer and a gentleman, viz. Socialism, Republicanism, Atheism, Art, and many other nameless vices. Also the Catacombs were, alas, no more, as their proprietor had taken himself to England to get a steady job. This meant that I was not seeing as much of Brendan as before. One day, I met Sally Travers, a niece of Micheál MacLiammoir's whom I knew well from working in the Gate, where she had played in her uncle's and Hilton Edwards's company. She told me of the play (still entitled *The Twisting of Another Rope*) which she said she had read when it had been submitted to Hilton some time previously. So I sought out Brendan and asked him for a copy.

It was some time before he was able to produce one for me, because it is very difficult, as any budding playwright will tell you, to get a manuscript back from any theatrical manager's office (including my own) once it has gone in. However, ultimately—I suppose it must have been some time in the middle of 1954—I got it into my possession. It was a rather unprepossessing document, typed with several different typewriters of various degrees of mechanical disintegration, on paper of varying shapes and sizes and dubious origins. I soon realized that this was for me. The construction was loose and in places, repetitious, but it was immediately clear to me that here was dialogue that could grip an audience and twist the emotions this way and that, as only O'Casey had done before.

Brendan proved an extremely co-operative author. This is by no means always the case with playwrights young or old. There are some who regard every word of their text in the same light that the more exuberant Protestant sects regard even the obscurest verses of the Bible. While no major rewriting was necessary, he permitted my wife to cut and rearrange various parts of the dialogue, and me to change the title.

Taking into consideration—as I did when naming the Pike—the fact that publicity accounts for a high proportion of the running costs of a small theatre, I felt that a title as long as *The Twisting of Another Rope* —visualized in terms of newspaper advertising rates— would make the economic disaster presaged by the huge cost of the play a certainty. It wasn't long before the phrase *The Quare Fellow*, which is the Dublin prison jargon for a condemned man, came to mind. Brendan had used it frequently throughout the play and it was both terse and interesting. As it happened, he was in London at the time, in connection with some newspaper work, and I phoned him there for permission to retitle the new play. To my delight, he agreed immediately.

While this was going on, we were running our second late night revue. The first, which had been our third show and had opened the previous Christmas, had been an enormous success. There were a number of reasons for its popularity. Firstly, intimate revue, as pioneered in England by the London Gate series, was new to the professional theatre in Dublin. Hilton Edwards had, before the war, run a very successful series of Christmas shows in the Dublin Gate, but they were not in the strict intimate revue tradition. They were really miscellaneous programmes of short playlets, Christmas songs and dramatic literary excerpts, such as MacLiammoir's spine-chilling version of Edgar Alan Poe's *The Cask of Amontillado*.

My wife, who, during the war years and after, had been an ardent Gingold-Baddeley fan, wrote this type of material very well, and I had learnt from Louis Elliman, managing director of the Gaiety Theatre and the Theatre Royal in Dublin, the important fact that in revue, you should not pause for applause at the end of every number, but bash straight on into the next item as quickly as it is physically possible to change the setting and bring on the new artist.

He had told me this some years previously when I was working for him in the Gaiety. Louis is a show business man *par excellence*. His idea of a successful show is to get as many star names as possible, regardless of their field, the maximum number of supporting artists, most elaborate scenery and the loudest musical combination he can find, and put them all on the biggest stage available.

This is not always a guarantee of artistic excellence. I was employed as stage director for one of these 3D technicolor, panoramic presentations, for which he had hired Hilton Edwards, Micheál MacLiammoir and a nucleus of the Gate Company; Noel Purcell, the Royalettes (the Dublin Theatre Royal 'Tiller Girls'), the chorus and soloists of the Dublin Grand Opera Society, and the Gaiety Orchestra; together with Babs de Monté, the costume designer from the Theatre Royal, and Carl Bonn, the stage designer from the Gate. Just for good measure was thrown in Max Moffat, a modelling engineer who had constructed a tubular steel giant about twenty feet high, which cost hundreds of pounds, and must have absorbed all the profits, if any, of the extravaganza. When he had contracted all these miscellaneous persons, he took himself off to the South of France, leaving me as stage director, the whipping-boy of all the warring factions. However, the point is that the lesson of speed learned under such Cecil B. de Mille conditions, when translated into the simple, speedily operated mechanisms of the Pike, meant that we could bang from one number into the next with such velocity that the audience had no chance to ponder on any deficiencies of material or performance.

It was in this revue that we had two Michaeál Mac-Liammoir's! *Othello* had been a favourite with Hilton and Micheál for a number of years. In their earlier productions, MacLiammoir always played Othello and Hilton Iago but, for a change this year, they decided to reverse the procedure, and my wife had the bright idea of a sketch made from the handker-chief jealousy scene, with Micheál playing both parts. This was achieved by using two actors, both of whom were capable of giving superb MacLiammoir imper-sonations. One of them was Godfrey Quigley, and the other, T. P. McKenna, who is now in the Abbey.

During the run of the revue, Dermot Kelly came to visit us. He had been with the Abbey some years previously, but had quarrelled with the management (in the best traditions of that theatre) and had suffered a period of exile in the fit-ups. He told me that he had heard I was doing a play by Brendan, and asked if I had a part for him. I was delighted, as Dermot is one of the finest character actors the Abbey, or indeed the country has ever produced, and ideally suited for the part of Neighbour in *The Quare Fellow*. After playing the part for me, he subsequently played it for the Associated-Rediffusion television version. He brought with him to my production of *The Quare Fellow*, the best traditions of the Abbey heyday, having spent his formative years in that theatre when the late F. J. McCormick was at the peak of his career; and I feel that I owe him a lot in the style of production I have developed.

I was a little bit worried about the possibly libellous aspect of *The Quare Fellow*. Brendan's great gift for colourful reportage meant that the astringent portraits of some of the Mountjoy warders seemed too good not to be true. However, I was by this time so enthusiastic about the play that I would allow nothing to interfere with my plans. In the event, nobody seems to have commented on this aspect of the show, even though it ran for four weeks in the Pike, in Theatre Workshop, the Comedy Theatre, two revivals in the Abbey, and the television version. I can only assume that either the characters of the various warders are a skilful amalgam of different individuals, or that any of them who were shown whole, as it were, were too self-conscious about the probability of ridicule to take any action.

Rehearsals, as always in the Pike with a large cast, were difficult. There were twenty-nine characters in the original play, which we reduced by doubling, to twenty-one. The number was reduced further in Theatre Workshop, which, I think, was a pity as it destroyed some of the continuity of characterization. This was particularly evident in the amalgamation made by Joan Littlewood of Donnelly and Warder One. Donnelly, in the original version, was the warder who opened the play. In the Stratford production, Warder Regan was given his lines at this point. They are, in fact, very different characters; Donnelly being a gruff, no-nonsense type of man, but essentially

44

decent and kindly. Regan, on the other hand, is a highly sensitive, almost neurotic Catholic; I might even say, if the imagination could reach to such a strange amalgam, a *New Statesman*-type Catholic. It is through Regan's mouth that Brendan gives us his own philosophy, and this does not match up at all with Donnelly's bluff, unthinking approach to life. I am glad to say that in the Abbey productions, and as far as I can remember, in the television one, this particular ha'porth of tar was not begrudged.

With such a large cast, it was necessary that I should use a number of amateurs and students for the production. In the choice of some of these part-time actors, I was very fortunate indeed. In particular, I remember Denis Hickie as Donnelly, and James Tinkler as the hangman. James Tinkler, in fact, was subsequently asked to take over from Christopher Casson in the first Abbey production, and Denis Hickie has played in many important Pike productions, both in our own little theatre and in the Gate and the Gaiety.

This brings me to a rather curious aspect of Dublin theatrical life. There are a couple of hundred full members of Irish Actors' Equity, and the economic problem of actors in Ireland is naturally one of the most important aspects of the work of the union. To reiterate the position; in Dublin, you have the Gaiety and Olympia Theatres, the Abbey and the Gate, and in Dun Laoghaire, the Gas Company. In addition, there is a new hundred-and-fifty-seater theatre, the Eblana, originally designed as a news cinema, in Michael Scott's Transport Centre, as well as a couple of sporadically operating pocket theatres, like the Pike.

The Gaiety has an annual schedule which goes something like this: from Christmas to the end of February, there is Jimmy O'Dea's pantomime, which is followed by a short season of plays by an Irish or visiting company. Then there is a season of amateur musicals, or opera presented by the Dublin Grand Opera Society, which employs visiting Italian, German, or English soloists singing with an amateur Dublin chorus. In the early summer, there is usually a locally-produced professional musical or visits from English touring musical companies like the D'Oyly Carte. In August, Jimmy O'Dea presents a family-type revue. This is usually followed by an autumn season with Irish or visiting professional play companies, before amateur musicals and the Dublin Grand Opera Society round off the time remaining before the panto season starts again. The pattern in the Olympia, though not quite so rigid, is much the same. The Gate gives a sort of continuous repertory of middle-to-highbrow plays, presented by a miscellany of companies, formerly including an occasional season of Lord Longford's own. Dun Laoghaire has, I am glad to say, been playing continuously with Irish professional companies for a number of years past.

All this means that work for professional actors outside the Abbey has been sporadic in the extreme. Commercial radio, which has developed over the last seven years or so, helps to keep the wolf from the door; but the prevailing circumstance usually means either a feast or a famine. Sometimes, if the Olympia and Gaiety are both presenting Irish professional companies, and the Gate and Dun Laoghaire have large casts, there is an acute shortage of pros in the city.

Other times, with amateur musicals or English tours in the large theatres, and small cast plays in the others, the situation is very much the reverse.

In London and, I imagine, New York, it is possible for actors to find fairly easily more-or-less congenial periodic employment in jobs of a non-theatrical nature, which can always be dropped if a part comes along. In Dublin, with its chronic unemployment, the situation is not so easy, and it is made more awkward by the fact that, with a small population, everybody knows everybody else's business. It would rather destroy the glamorous aspect of the theatre, if you saw last week's Hamlet pulling pints as a temporary barman at your local—an activity quite practicable in the anonymity of a huge city.

The tendency, therefore, among a lot of talented acting potential in Dublin, is to obtain a steady job in the Civil Service, or other not too exacting, pension dispensing large organization, and to work as frequently as possible at night in the theatre, taking annual leave when the exigencies of rehearsals make it necessary to be on stage during the day-time. As a matter of fact, the late Barry Fitzgerald and several other famous Irish actors started in this way. It does not, however, make for tranquil and efficient rehearsal periods, and is resented by those actors brave enough not to provide themselves with any other means of support.

When I was on the Executive of Irish Actor's Equity, we thrashed this problem out at some length, and the solution which seemed to us the most workable has been in operation ever since. It is the system of having a Union Shop (as opposed to a Closed Shop) and insisting on all actors, save a small percentage of students, being paid a minimum salary to prevent the part-timer undercutting the pro. For example, you are rehearsing a play demanding eight-hour daily rehearsals. A, a full-time professional, and B, a man with another job, apply for a part. The natural tendency is to give the part to A so that the rehearsal schedule may be maintained, since they both cost the same. It is, of course, only a stopgap solution, and doesn't really make for happy relations in the theatre; but as yet, neither Equity nor any Dublin management, have succeeded in finding a better answer to the problem.

All this may seem a little irrelevant but, in fact, it should help to give the reader some sort of an idea of the economic theatrical background which initiated Brendan Behan and, in earlier years, Sean O'Casey. Nowadays, the Abbey has a nucleus of about twenty artists, continuously on salary or small retainer, which is made possible by the fact that they have a permanent state subsidy. From time to time, however, when doing a very large cast play, even they have to call in outsiders, and certainly at the time when O'Casey was having his first big triumph, the situation there was much as it is in the other Dublin theatres today.

In England and America, playwrights nowadays have tended to write their plays bearing in mind the economics, first of Broadway and the West End, and secondly, of the small professional repertory and stock companies which formed the economic backbone of the English-speaking theatre between the wars. As I have pointed out, with the elastic meaning of the word 'professional' as applied in the early Abbey, such tight-fisted restrictions on the playwright's imagination did not apply. Consequently, the tradition of large casts has been strong in Ireland. This often makes it difficult for a play to be adequately cast abroad, and partly explains why O'Casey, considering his stature in world dramaturgy is so rarely performed outside Ireland. The only other Irish playwrights to have made a really solid impact on world theatre are Beckett, with *Waiting for Godot* (four men and a boy) and Brendan, who has had his plays performed mostly under the auspices of Theatre Workshop, where a no-star policy seems to have made the presentation of large cast plays economically feasible.

One other point worth mentioning is this connection is the economic cycle of a play in Ireland, as opposed to that in England or America, where try-out, West End and repertory performances (in that order) seem to be the normal pattern. In Ireland, the financial pinnacle of a play's career is the royalty from its presentation in the Abbey. This, after a suitable interval, is followed by a steady income from amateur performances throughout the length and breadth of Ireland, where, apart from an extraordinarily high number of amateur presentations of a routine nature, the market has been boosted by an interlocking network of competitive amateur drama festivals, culminating in an All-Ireland Final. Therefore, proportionate to the population as a whole (four million odd for the thirty-two counties) the financial return to the author on a play which has had any sort of success in the Abbey or one of the large Dublin theatres, may be quite reasonable, even though it never crosses the sea in any direction.

Brendan was delighted with rehearsals. It has been my privilege to launch the first plays of four or five Irish writers, and it is always a source of amusement and satisfaction to me to watch their incredulous expressions the first time they hear their lines spoken by the cast. Brendan was no exception. In fact, he retained a naïve pleasure in hearing his work performed, for many years, though I dare say nowadays, with first nights in London, Paris, Berlin and New York behind him, the wonder of it may have worn off a bit.

Dublin, though it has most of the attributes of a capital city, also maintains a certain village-like quality, and it wasn't long before word got around that there was something exciting brewing in the Pike. How this happens, I don't know exactly, but I have never put on anything good in Dublin when word didn't get around beforehand and there wasn't an eager anticipation of success which gives the first nights a sense of real excitement and occasion. I find this a very great contrast to London, where there are so many first nights, and the *habitués*, cynical to the effulgencies of the advance publicity of the press representatives, sit rigid in their stalls, their basilisk eyes fixed on the curtain with a cold determination to put author, producer and actors to the arduous test of their most clinical scrutiny.

Of course, Dublin goes to the other extreme, and to the untrained ear, the loyal enthusiasm of friends and well-wishers can seem like a guarantee of world-wide success. I well remember the first night of

5(a). Scene from Act I of *The Quare Fellow*.

5(b). Another scene from Act I of *The Quare Fellow*.

6. Samuel Beckett.

O'Casey's *The Bishop's Bonfire*. The London critics had all flocked to Dublin to see the master's first new work for some years performed in the Gaiety Theatre. Due to the exigencies of the deadline, a number of English dailies had been permitted to attend the dress rehearsal, after which they had written their main copy. During the interval, on the first night, they trooped out to their telephones and, intoxicated by the boisterously enthusiastic reception, hurried to dictate some extra superlatives to their London offices. The next morning, after the Irish critics, some reluctantly, some with relish, had damned the play, I chanced on a bunch of the visitors, headed by Cookman and Darlington, in the Shelbourne Hotel, where I had been brought by an English journalist to meet a colleague. 'Well, you've made nice fools of us!' said Cookman, amazed and horrified that such a triumphant first night could mean so little.

As the momentous day drew nearer, the atmosphere became too much for Brendan and he took solidly to the bottle, appearing at intervals accompanied by some friendly but uncomprehending soak whom he had acquired in his perambulations through the various pubs in the area. The latter, puzzled as to why he had been dragged away from his creamy pint to this strange, cold garage in a back lane, would sit in the auditorium, muttering amiable obscenities, while Brendan dug him in the ribs and repeated again and again, 'I wrote that!' The climax was reached at the dress rehearsal, when the author arrived with only sufficient equilibrium to last him to the door of the theatre. He then collapsed in a heap on the floor, and

I had to have him lifted on to the back seat, where he reclined, resplendently comitose, for the entire length of the play. The friendly but persistent complaints from the cast that they could not hear each other's lines, made it necessary for me to detail an assistant stage manager to sit beside our pride and hope, and shake him every time his snores rendered the dialogue inaudible.

The first night itself was exciting. The Behan family was there in strength, as were all the Dublin critics. What remaining room there was in the tiny theatre was packed. The editor of the *Irish Press*, determined to do his protégé well, and being unable, for one reason or another, to send his regular number one critic, sought around for some distinguished man of letters to send in his place. His choice fell, rather unfortunately, on the late Dr. Lennox Robinson, who was at that time one of the directors of the Abbey responsible for the selection of plays. During one of the intervals, Gabriel Fallon, now himself a director of the Abbey, but then critic for the *Dublin Evening Press* (and incidentally, one of the play's most enthusiastic supporters), turned to Lennox and said, 'Well, Lennox; how are you liking it?' 'My dear fellow,' moaned the lank, bespectacled doyen of the Irish theatrical revival, 'how can you possibly expect me to enjoy a play I turned down?'

I had been worried throughout the performance, not so much by the possible artistic imperfections of my production, but by what the ribald exuberance of the author might lead him to say or do, after or during the show. Because, whatever facilities they may or may not have in Stratford East for dealing with

Brendan's Rabelasian comment and curtain-call ora-
tory, the fifty-five-seater Pike, with its telephone-
kiosk foyer, filled as it was with a mixed company of
comparatively straight-laced Dubliners, offered no
means for the muffling of irregularities, either vocal
or physical.

During the intervals, Tom Willoughby, the manager (in between brief appearances as the Governor of
Mountjoy), my wife, whom Brendan regards with a
mixture of terror and affection, and Rosamond
Stevens, Tom's wife and the theatre's public relations
officer, kept Brendan in a delicately balanced state of
intoxication, scientifically planned by Stephen Behan
to maintain him in a condition where he would not
get so dry as to be tempted to wander off in search of
further supplies, thereby missing the final curtain,
nor, on the other hand, become so ossified that he
wouldn't be able to stand upright to receive whatever
plaudits might be forthcoming. This manœuvre succeeded admirably, and apart from an occasional shout
of encouragement to the cast, which they received
with equanimity—having expected far worse—he
conducted himself with reasonable composure during
the performance.

'I wouldn't say very much after the show,' I suggested tentatively. 'Oh, God, no, I'd be terrified. I'll
tell you what I'll do, I'll sing a song.' So to a surprised
and delighted audience, he gave a good, if alcoholic
rendering of Sean O'Casey's 'Red Roses for Me',
which was received with general acclaim, except for
the critic of the *Evening Herald*, who tut-tutted mildly
about it in his review.

After the show there was a hilarious and melodious

party in the best Behan tradition, which went on well into the small hours. My last recollections of that night were Tom, Rosamond and myself wandering unsteadily from newspaper office to newspaper office, feverishly purchasing edition after edition of the morning papers until ultimately we obtained the city editions containing the long-awaited notices. Our hasty perusal of the still damp print showed us that we had got excellent criticisms in the *Irish Times* and the *Independent*, but that Dr. Lennox's loyalty to the editor of the *Irish Press* only made him conceal his distaste by fulsome praise for the actors.

The Irish papers, almost without exception, hailed the new play as, to quote the *Irish Independent*, 'the finest new play by a new dramatist seen in Dublin for some years', and Gabriel Fallon wrote, 'Our academicians of drama may dismiss Mr. Behan's work on the grounds of technical immaturity, may suggest cutting this, tightening up that; but Mr. Behan has what most of our academicians lack, an abundance of felt life, and when he has found himself technically, the Irish Theatre will have found another and I think, a greater, O'Casey.' Even Dr. Robinson finished up by, 'Just for the acting alone, it is a play which must be seen and seen again.' The only really dissident note was struck by the *Evening Herald*. The reason for his disapproval may possibly be found in the closing words of his criticism, which were, 'The play, it may be added, was observed in circumstances of much discomfort, due to overcrowding'.

A slightly amusing (in retrospect) contretemps during the run, not normal to most theatrical enterprises, was the calling out on twenty-four-hour duty of myself and the stage carpenter and electrician, Edmund Kelly, who was also in the Army. A member of the cast volunteered to handle the tricky lighting plot, and my wife and the Willoughbys performed the various functions normally carried out by myself, while Ned and I, in our respective capacities as section sergeant and second-in-command of the Second Field Engineers, slaved through the night, blasting chunks out of an embankment in an endeavour to alleviate the flooding caused by the swollen Tolka River at the North Strand, not far from Mountjoy Jail. I wonder if the prisoners, hearing the explosions, thought that the new revolution had come at last.

We were only able to play for four weeks, because, first of all, as I have said, many of the small parts were played by amateurs who couldn't stay with us for a longer period, and also, despite the packed theatre, and the fact that some of the artists were unpaid, the expenses exceeded the income by approximately ten shillings per week.

After the completion of the run, we quickly organized another late-night revue in order to try and make some money as, except for *Waiting for Godot*, all the straight plays presented resulted in a loss. Also, wishing to make some more royalties for Brendan and some profits for ourselves, we set about looking for a larger theatre in which to revive *The Quare Fellow*. This proved impossible because we could not get any of the large theatres in Dublin to give us a letting. It was partly prejudice against a small, rather revolutionary group, working in a back lane, and partly against Brendan himself, whose alcoholic and proletarian background made the more 'respectable' managements feel that there must be something dubious about a play written by such a person, and launched in a garage. In fact, one management gave as the reason that Brendan's brother, once employed by them as gallery spot operator in their theatre, had been fired for selling the *Daily Worker* to gallery patrons during working hours, and that they wouldn't dream of having a play in their theatre connected with such a family. However, I believe the reason has something to do with the sort of snivelling inferiority complex that even today affects the Irish Establishment class, which for all its 'Patriotism' believes that nothing is good unless it comes from London. Because it was not until *The Quare Fellow* had been successful in Stratford and the West End that the Abbey saw fit to present the play. Mind you, I remember meeting, at a London cocktail party, the wife of a well-known West End theatre manager, who remarked to me *apropos* of the new wave of 'dustbin' plays, that 'one is almost afraid to bring one's friends to one's own theatre these days. One never knows *what* one will see!'

Having failed to secure a large-scale Dublin production, we set about trying to interest a London management in the play, but were pipped at the post by Joan Littlewood and Jerry Raffles, her able and fast-moving chief of staff. This caused a falling out between Brendan and ourselves, because we felt resentful at his having given it to Theatre Workshop behind our backs; while he could not see why his play, so highly praised by the Irish critics, should languish in the drawer of a London theatre manager's office instead of bringing him a reasonable financial return. Actually this happens to a lot of plays, an example being *Waiting for Godot*, which was knocked around, the subject of proposition and counter-proposition, for about two years before its 1955 production in the Arts Theatre.

With typical spontaneous Behan generosity, however, after enjoying our staging of the first professional presentation in English of Sartre's *Nekrassov* at the Gate Theatre, Brendan gave us a handsome contribution to our funds and subsequently has helped us in many ways both financially and otherwise.

I didn't, for obvious reasons, have anything to do with Brendan's subsequent rocketing to his present position as major playwright and pressman's meal ticket, but for those who may not be familiar with his career, I will try to summarize his later adventures. In Dublin, before *The Quare Fellow* was presented, he had already become well known through his writings in the Irish Press, and while the prudish and the starchy have always and will always disapprove of him, he was held in considerable affection by both workers and intellectuals. But it was his now almost historic appearance on Malcolm Muggeridge's B.B.C. television programme that first drew him to the attention of the public outside Ireland.

What happened was really quite simple. The B.B.C. apparently has a custom of providing its interviewees with a drink to steady their nerves before such an appearance and, as far as I can gather, Brendan was left more or less on his own with a bottle of whiskey for some time before the scheduled time of transmission. In dealing with an explorer just returned from the Amazon, a distinguished art expert, or with any other of the average-type celebrities normally seen on this sort of programme, this is probably both a wise and a hospitable procedure. What the B.B.C. probably didn't realize was that Brendan, basically a shy man for all his apparent flamboyance, had already been fortifying himself elsewhere, and the B.B.C.'s bottle was the last straw for a camel masochistically eager to have its back broken.

Things didn't go right from the start. I understand that Mr. Muggeridge was in the habit of lighting a cigarette for himself immediately before appearing on camera, in order to give the proceedings a relaxed note. Brendan, just about able to stand at this point, shattered Muggeridge's equilibrium by taking the lighted cigarette from his fingers a second before the camera turned on them, in a further attempt to calm his own jangled nerves. The effort of this sudden movement must have been too much for him, for by the time Muggeridge had recovered his composure sufficiently to start the interview, Brendan was past comprehensible speech and answered his questioner with grunts and incoherent mumbles.

One of the British public's greatest sources of delight and righteous indignation is when the British Broadcasting Corporation blots its copy-book. There had not been such a rumpus since the pre-war 'the Fleet's all lit up' incident, when a commentator describing a Royal Naval Review was more lit up than the scene he was talking about. I wonder if it is a comment on the age we live in that the one sure way to gain public interest, and to draw favourable attention to one's artistic activities, is to behave in some way that is generally considered out-rageous.

Certainly, from that moment, Brendan's every movement became the eager concern of Fleet Street, and whenever he was in London to attend a per-formance of his plays, or indeed for any other reason, he was followed wherever he went by a horde of eager newshounds, some of whom were unscrupulous enough to load him deliberately with alcohol, in order to produce copy. It says a lot for Brendan's strength of character that he has remained largely un-spoilt by treatment which would make another in-sufferable. Since his illness, however, I have noticed a tendency among his real friends in the journalist profession (and indeed he has many) to protect him from this sort of thing.

After its six months at the Comedy Theatre, *The Quare Fellow* was presented at the Abbey. I was quite moved by the experience of sitting with Stephen and Kathleen, watching their son stand on the stage of the Queen's Theatre, which once had been managed by P. J. Bourke, Kathleen's brother-in-law. The first production of the play in the Abbey suffered in my view very much from the absence of Dermot Kelly in the part of Neighbour, but this was remedied in a later presentation when Ray MacAnally gave a fine, though completely different, interpretation of this part.

By this time Brendan was married to Beatrice Salkeld, daughter of the Irish artist, Cecil Salkeld, and grand-daughter of the poetess Blanaid Salkeld. Several times I had noticed Brendan with this quiet girl, who is herself an excellent painter, but was amazed when

I heard of the marriage, as I didn't really regard Brendan as the marrying type, or Beatrice as courageous enough to take on the responsibility of such an explosive husband. However, not many people have the opportunity of testing the marriage vows, 'For richer, for poorer; in sickness and in health' quite so thoroughly, and I may say the Brendan Behans seem well set towards following the fine example of Stephen and Kathleen.

The Hostage had quite an interesting history, which I believe is not very widely known. The organization dedicated to the revival of the Irish language which has had most success in recent years is Gael Linn. They are provided with ample funds from a football pool run for the purpose, and they do not believe in any form of cheese paring which is so frequently the hallmark of Irish Government efforts to foster Gaelic. Nothing, they feel, but the best in personnel and material should be utilized in gaining their ends of popularizing and furthering the Irish language and way of life. Also they do not suffer from the straight-laced prudery, which seemed a few years ago to have gone hand in hand with the Gaelic revival. This was epitomized in the public mind in Ireland by a young man in sober tweeds, his lapel decorated with a gold fáinne and the Sacred Heart pin of the Pioneer Total Abstinence Association, stiffly dancing a sexless jig with a bespectacled, thick stockinged, tweedy young woman.

Anyway, shortly after the success of *The Quare Fellow*, Gael Linn commissioned Brendan to write them a play in Irish. *An Gáill* (*The Hostage*) was performed to packed houses in their little Irish-language theatre in St. Stephen's Green. The good-natured blasphemy and mockery of extreme nationalism and other absurdities of Irish life went largely uncriticized at this performance, whereas when the English production was seen lately in the very theatre which had, a bare five years previously, refused a hearing to the author's first play, it was greeted with shocked protests from the patriotic patrons, who had apparently been not sufficiently versed in their own language to see it in its original version.

Chapter III

SAMUEL BECKETT

~~~~~~

IF BRENDAN BEHAN could be said to be a highly-coloured representative specimen of the Dublin worker exemplifying, in a magnified form, many of their virtues as well as the other thing, Samuel Beckett in some ways personifies the *bourgeois*, well-to-do Protestant, Trinity College background from which he springs. That is not to say for a minute, though, that either of them can be remotely regarded as typical of their youthful environment.

They are about as different as two people could possibly be, while at the same time retaining certain qualities, essentially Irish in origin, which seem common to both. Where Brendan, with the traditional logic inherited from generations living on an uncertain weekly wage, will be unbelievably generous when the wherewithal for generosity is at hand, Sam's actions are at all times guided by the almost pedantic sense of straightforward honesty which is one of the virtues of the Protestant heritage. Although as technicians they are as different as a few pints in Mooney's after Mass is from the ritual of the Protestant Sunday lunch, yet their work bears the common quality of a penetrating yet warm-hearted humanity.

Both authors in private life are men of very strong character. They do what they want, how they want, when they want. In Brendan's case this is concealed under an effervescent 'blarney'; in Sam's, under a gentle charm. I am sure, however, that Brendan's superiors in the I.R.A. found him somewhat of a handful, and it has been said that a thesis of Sam Beckett's for some post-graduate examination in Trinity was submitted on lavatory paper. Nonconforming yet conforming, Samuel Beckett was in the first eleven of the Dublin University Cricket Club, though it is only fair to state that Brendan Behan played hooker for the first Rugby XV of Hollesley Bay Borstal Institution.

The Dublin of 1927, which was when Sam graduated, bore little relationship to the Dublin of today. Trinity College, Ballsbridge, the Viceregal Lodge (with a Governor-General instead of a Viceroy) were still socially and philosophically much as they had been under the Westminster government. The Dublin of the literary *salons* and good conversation, of Oliver Gogarty, of Yeats (then at the height of his powers and living in a large house by Merrion Square) was in full swing. The Dublin of Joyce's Mr. Bloom, even, still existed in a measure, despite the superficial political and social changes brought about by the war and the technical demise of British rule.

It was this Dublin that the young egghead left to take up a position as Reader of English in the École Normale Supériore in Paris and, in 1930, the legendary post-war patron of *avant-garde* literature, Lady Cunard, published his long poem 'Whoroscope'.

Apart from a year in Trinity in 1931, as lecturer in French (a post now held by our mutual friend, Dr. A. J. Leventhal, who incidentally probably knows more about Beckett and his writing than anyone else in the world) his time spent in Dublin has been purely as a visitor, his last sojourn of any length being in 1954, when he came to nurse his brother during his fatal illness.

This rejection in his twenties of Ireland as a domicile, has enabled him to attain the detachment from any environment which is necessary to the making of plays out of purely abstract themes, as has also his rejection of the language of his upbringing. Apart from plays commissioned by the B.B.C., the last occasion on which he wrote a major work initially in English was in 1944, when his novel *Watt* was completed.[1]

There is in Paris an atmosphere conducive to detachment, both in writing and other art forms, but I think that Sam Beckett can be said to be less 'involved' than any of his contemporaries or successors in the field of playwriting.

In fact, although most of his friends in Paris today are politically committed one way or another, and many of them have signed the famous Manifeste des Cent Vingt-et-un,[2] he feels that not being a French citizen morally forbids him from expressing any public or even private opinions on these matters. I asked him about his period in the Resistance.

'That was different,' he said, 'I was fighting against

---

[1] His latest play *Happy Days* is written in English.

[2] A document written by Sartre and signed by one hundred and twenty one intellectuals. It supported the F.L.N. in Algeria.

the Germans, who were making life hell for my friends, and not for the French nation.'

In Ireland, as in any country, the population can be pretty neatly divided into categories. I don't use the word 'classes' because the religious issue in Ireland makes straightforward classification complicated. However, as I will be dealing with this in a later chapter, it is easier now to try and analyse the various influences and environments that have been directly at work on the character of the author of *En Attendant Godot*.

Like myself, his earliest education was in one of the dozen or so private Protestant day schools in Dublin. With the decline of the Protestant population, brought about by the removal of British influence, only a few of them remain. In Sam's case, his first school probably meant more in his life than my own did in mine, for he was at Earlsford House, which in those days was run by a Frenchman called Lepelon, who gave him his interest in the French language. It is this interest which has affected him, not merely in the material sense, in that it has enabled him to go to France and work, but also in the sense that it is the basis of his interest in pure abstract philosophy. This differentiates him from, say, someone like Shaw who, although also a Protestant Dubliner, spent all his formative years in Dublin and London, and whose intellectual energy seems always to have been expressed in terms of what one might call the practical, day-to-day political philosophy, which is perhaps the hall-mark of the British as opposed to the French approach to life. The French are perfectionists, who seek the Absolute Solution to any problem, whereas the British, we are told, are always prepared to Muddle Through. Let it be said, however, that if the French ideal isn't found, the attempts to attain it can lead to a greater shambles than the British method.

Like myself, the next stage in Sam's education was a trip north to a Protestant public school. It was Portora Royal School, Enniskillen, which though much older, was not unlike Campbell College, Belfast, where I went, and where Sam was to spend two terms after graduating in Trinity as French master. He still retains to this day, despite his gentle nature and the liberalizing influence of life in intellectual Paris, a slightly astringent quality, reminiscent of a North of Ireland pedant.

Portora was, in those days at least, a pretty tough environment for a young boy coming straight from the well-ordered comfort of a Dublin day-school-existence: long runs before breakfast, compulsory rugger and cricket, and the traditionally hearty life of an English-type public school. This must surely offer an enormous contrast to the school-days of his French friends and fellow-writers. Although he was not happy at first, it wasn't long before he adjusted himself to the new life, and his interest in the French language, awakened in his day school, was fostered by the French teacher, Miss Tennant.

One of the curiosities which the new boy at Portora noticed was the impressive Roll of Honour of scholars of the school; on the left, the date, on the right, the name. Opposite one of the dates there was a painted blank. I believe the name has since been written in again. It is Oscar Wilde. I suspect that the discovery of the reasons for effacing the name of such

7. The supply of bowler hats.

8. Scene from *Men without Shadows.*

an important Old Boy from the school, combined with his later friendship with Joyce and the knowledge of the latter's treatment by his fellow-countrymen, has had a very strong influence on his thinking and writing. Certainly, for such a mild-mannered and essentially upright man, he seems to have a fixation with the less attractive aspects of physical life, combined with an almost adolescent awareness of his right to shock.

Among his early works, a study of Proust was sandwiched between *Whoroscope* and a collection of short stories entitled *More Pricks than Kicks*.

English and Irish puritanical prejudices, particularly the latter, seem constantly in his mind. He wrote to me in 1953: '. . . I think you had better read the play before we go any further. I have translated it myself into English, as literally as I could, and am now revising this translation for American publication in the Spring. Frankly, I cannot see how an integral performance would be possible in Dublin, even in such a theatre as yours, because of certain crudities of language, if for no better reason; and I would not consent to their being changed or removed . . . if finally you feel you can undertake to put on the play as it stands, there should be no difficulty about permission.' He told me recently that he had been authorized some time ago to make discreet inquiries in Dublin as to whether it would be acceptable to have Joyce's remains transferred, as Yeats's were, to Dublin, for official reinterment in his native land; and I felt that I detected the slightest touch of perverse pleasure when he was able to tell me that the answer had been in the negative.

Back in Dublin again, at Trinity, he came under two very important influences. One was Professor Rudmose Brown, whose assistant he was later to become, and the other was the Abbey Theatre, which he attended regularly. The latter connection may come as a surprise to those who, like a young American post-graduate student who recently sought my advice on a thesis she was writing about Beckett, don't particularly connect his writing with the land of his birth. People who have only seen or read his plays outside Ireland, never seem to realize quite how 'Irish' his dialogue is, though this was recognized in the production at the Royal Court of *End Game*, by the casting of an Irish actor, Jack McGowran, in the part of Clov. But Sam has never been a great theatregoer in France, and I suspect he unconsciously visualizes his characters in terms of the great Abbey actors of his student days: Barry FitzGerald, F. J. McCormick and so on. He himself says that he was influenced by J. M. Synge, but his dialogue flows best in the Dublinese which, in heightened form, is the language of O'Casey and of Brendan Behan.

Under the guidance of Rudmose Brown, he became a first-class student of French literature, and the professor arranged for him to take up a Readership in English at the École Normale Supérieure. When he had completed his appointed spell in Paris, Rudmose Brown brought him back to Trinity as his assistant. However, the academic life didn't suit him and, at the end of his first year, while wandering on the Continent during the Long Vac., he suddenly and without warning posted his resignation to the University. His Protestant conscience has troubled him

ever since. He had agreed to three years, he had completed one. Perhaps it was this, combined with the
recognition by his old University of his place in the
world of letters, when they bestowed on him an Hon-
orary Degree, that prompted him to donate all royalties from *Krapp's Last Tape* to Trinity College funds.

A year after he renounced the academic life, his
father (who was a quantity surveyor and partner in
the firm, Beckett and Metcalfe, Clare Street, Dublin)
died, leaving him two hundred a year. It has been on
this, supplemented by meagre literary earnings, that
he has lived until his comparatively recent theatrical
successes have enabled him to indulge in a new apart-
ment, a country cottage two hours' drive from Paris,
and a Citroen Deux Chevaux.

After leaving Trinity and becoming involved in
continental philosophy, he came under the influence
of Jules Romains (author of *Dr. Knock*), whose now
defunct philosophic school of 'Unanimism' was based
on the study of group psychology and was an attempt
to explain away religion and religious phenomena.
By 1937, he finally settled in Paris, although he was
still writing in English, and his first novel, *Murphy*,
was published by Routledges in 1938; 1939 found
him on one of his infrequent visits to Dublin. By this
time, most of his close friends lived in Paris and he
hurried back there at the outbreak of war and, by
1940, was up to his neck in the Resistance movement.

Paris became more and more difficult. Count
O'Kelly (the Irish Minister in Paris) offered Joyce an
Irish passport, which the embittered Dubliner refused
even though it would have eased the hardships that
he knew he would have to suffer in order to try and

make his way to Switzerland and safety. Indeed his secretary, Paul Léon, was dragged off by the Gestapo and killed *en route* to a concentration camp. Incidentally, many people believe that Beckett did secretarial work for Joyce, but in fact what he did was to read to him and take dictation, like a number of that unhappy author's friends, after blindness had made reading and writing impossible for him.

Swiss regulations demanded that immigrants possess what for Joyce was a very large sum of money, so he made his way painfully to the Unoccupied Zone of France, where he and his family eked out a precarious existence. By the time he had collected the necessary funds, he was a very sick man, and was only to live a few weeks in the neutral haven of Zurich.

These sad events leading up to the miserable and exiled death of a writer so greatly revered among men of letters throughout the world, still further strengthened Beckett's dislike of Irish puritanical Catholicism, and the narrow-minded prudery of the Philistine Irish and English conventionalists.

For the next couple of years, he was fully occupied with Resistance activities which did not leave much time for work on the novel *Watt*, which was to be his last publication in English for some time to come. Agents brought information, verbally and written on miscellaneous scraps of paper, ranging from bus tickets upwards, which it was his job to sort, classify and type. They were then microphotoed and sent to Allied Headquarters in England. He modestly assumes that they were of little or no importance, and I dare say only a careful perusal of the relative archives of the period could prove or disprove the

fact. However, the risks were enormous and ultimately the inevitable happened. Just as in Sartre's
play, *Men without Shadows*, one of the group was
caught by the Gestapo, and within a couple of hours,
Sam and Suzanne were on the run. After enduring
all the dangers and vicissitudes depicted in so many
novels and films of the Resistance, they succeeded in
reaching the Unoccupied Zone, where he worked as
a farm labourer and completed *Watt*. Shortly after
the end of hostilities in Europe, the Irish Red Cross
set up a hospital in Saint Lô, and he joined the staff
there, as storekeeper and interpreter.

In 1947, he returned to Paris and started writing
again in earnest, this time in French. He is a painstaking writer, first working in longhand and then
typing several drafts before he is satisfied. I was rather
interested to learn that he finds a play much easier to
write than a novel. I find this particularly surprising,
because I have always considered that a play was the
most difficult of all literary work. The possible explanation is that, for a man like Beckett, who works
so much in the abstract and with no handy plot
formula to guide him, the inevitable restriction and
discipline of the theatre and the spoken word is a
help rather than a hindrance. *Godot* was written in a
month, and he has responded far more easily than
most authors of his distinction to the additional disciplines imposed by radio.

All that Fall and *Embers* could be used as standard
examples in any school of radio writing and the fact
that *Embers* won the Italia prize emphasizes the point.
Many producers, including myself, have sought his
permission to perform these plays on the stage, and

he has always refused to allow it. He has used in all his writing, the element of mystery and doubt as an aid to creating his images. In *Embers* the man sits on the beach. We hear the crunch of the pebbles as he sits down. Later we hear the wife's voice, but do not hear any corresponding sound effect. Is she there, in fact, or is her voice merely in the imagination? We do not know. We are not supposed to know.

En Attendant Godot was not his first play. His first was called *Eleutheria*, and was about two places represented by two sides of a stage, one in darkness, the other in light. Activities in both places. Then the lighting is reversed.

On its completion, Suzanne (now Mme Beckett) started to hawk *Godot* and *Eleutheria* around the Paris managements. No one was interested. However, after the manuscripts had reposed in the files of Jean Vilar's Théâtre Nationale Populaire for some time, she was informed that *Eleutheria* might be presented in a one-act form. Beckett would not consider this, and she continued her peregrinations until she was advised to see Roger Blin, who was director and administrator of the Gaieté-Montparnasse. National Theatres (French *or* Irish) should, it seems, be avoided by adventurous authors until they have made their names elsewhere.

Time passed, as is usual in these matters and then, while Blin was playing in Adamov's *La Grande et le petit Manœuvre* at the Noctambules Theatre, Beckett was introduced to him. Blin told him that he liked *En Attendant Godot* and would like to put it on. This he was not able to do until Serreau offered him the opportunity in his newly constructed Théâtre de

Babylone, and the opening took place a year later, in January 1953. It is interesting to note that the management were the recipients of a state grant worth the equivalent of £600, which is payable by the French Government to anyone presenting the first production of a first play of any author writing in the French language. I am afraid it was not without envy that I heard this fact.

The newspaper criticisms set a standard of disagreement that was to be followed in the English-speaking world. The popular press, such as *France Soir* was unfavourable, except where the acting was concerned. *Figaro* compared the author with Kafka, Joyce and Flaubert, but said that the play was not for the general public. The reaction of *Arts* on the 22nd January 1953, was not unlike the subsequent reaction of the 'posh English Sundays', but in rather more high-flown language:

'. . . A perfect work that deserves a triumph. I will not tell you the plot. Would one describe a landscape, a face a drawing or an emotion? . . .'

(Needless to say, they went on to try and describe the plot!) The Catholic paper, *La Croix*, described it as the most interesting new play of the season, and *L'Observateur* of the 8th January 1953, referring to the play's tranquil despair, said: 'It was not considered until now a good subject for the theatre,' and went on to say how tricky it was to use the theme of boredom without boring the audience. *Nouvelles Littéraires* compared Beckett with Adamov and Ionesco, and expressed the opinion that he was much better in this particular field of writing than those two authors.

Just as in England, Harold Hobson and Kenneth Tynan kept referring to *Godot* week after week, so *Figaro Littéraire* seemed unable to leave the subject alone, and kept up a constant discussion in its pages throughout the play's run. Even ordinary reporters did not seem to be able to keep their pens off *Godot*. One of these accosted Arthur Miller, who happened to be visiting Paris at the time, and asked him whether he had seen the play. To translate more or less literally, the report runs: 'His eyes shone with retrospective satisfaction as he said: "Oh, it's a very good play!"' An interesting sidelight on the French passion for critical classification of their writers was an article on 'L'Humour Noire' where Beckett was compared to Henri Michaux.

Meanwhile, in Dublin, the work of converting 18A Herbert Lane into the Pike Theatre Club was proceeding. The Herbert Street house, of which the Pike was originally the coach-house, is now occupied by the French Cultural Centre, and they used to permit us to use the tiny garden which linked the two buildings, for dyeing canvas and other jobs too awkward to be carried out inside the theatre. I discovered from the librarian, with whom we used to gossip during the rests between building activities, that she was a keen Beckett fan, and so I wrote the letter referred to in Chapter I.

Our first production in the 'Pike', carefully chosen for its prestige value and 'suitability', was the world première of a play by G. K. Chesterton, written six years before his death. The reason we had been able to obtain the rights so easily was apparent after the opening night. The play was charming in its way, but dull as ditchwater, and I am afraid not very well done. The minds of the audience and critics were bored stiff as their behinds from our new seating, and the notices damned us with faint praise.

I realized that something a bit more stimulating would have to be dug up if our new venture was to be a success. I therefore enlisted the help of Dr. Leventhal in persuading Sam to give us the rights of *Godot*, a script of which we had received from Paris. In his letter to us, telling us we could do the play, Beckett said at the end, 'You had better, as a matter of courtesy, inform my London agents of your plans'.

Thinking this a mere formality, we wrote gaily to London, telling them that we proposed to present the play the following year. We were horrified to receive an apologetic but firm note from London, informing us that they could not consider granting us permission to present the play in Dublin, as they were hoping for a London production. This depressed us, but we carried on with our immediate plans, which took us well into the following summer. Cheered by the success of our spring season, we decided we could manage a short trip to Paris in June. I don't know at what stage it was when, worrying over the problem of how to bring *Godot* to the Pike, I started to wonder whether in fact the London agents had any right to prevent us going ahead with a Dublin production. Anyway, I decided to try and have a look at the contract while I was there.

To my delight, on reading it, I found that the English language section specifically covered, on the one part, the U.S.A. and Canada, and on the other, the British Commonwealth of Nations. In 1948, the Prime Minister of the Irish Coalition Government then in power, in an attempt to 'take the gun out of politics' and to placate the extreme Republican wing of his Cabinet, had declared the Republic of Ireland and had seceded from the British Commonwealth. This historic occasion had passed unnoticed by the London agents, and I realized there was nothing to stop us presenting the play, provided Sam would stand over his original permission. The Summer Revue, the world premiére of *The Quare Fellow* and the Christmas Revue, seemed to make the following spring (1955), the ideal moment for presenting the play. Beckett agreed, and we continued with the production of *The Quare Fellow*, described in the last chapter, mentally cocking a snook at the helpless potentates of London's West End.

There was a good deal of shilly-shallying about the production in London. The London rights were held jointly by Peter Glenville and Donald Albery. Glenville, I believe, visualized the play in terms of stars of the calibre of Sir Ralph Richardson, but for one reason or another, things didn't work out for him. In the meantime, Sam asked us to hold our horses for a bit because, while it was clear that he was perfectly within his rights to let us go ahead, there was obviously so much money involved in the London production that it would have been disastrous if we had irritated them to the point of losing their already not very firm resolve to put on the play. However, ultimately Mr. Glenville retired from the scene of action and Donald Albery decided to go ahead with a production in the Arts Theatre Club, without the publicity assistance of big stars. By this time, it was autumn 1955.

It may encourage those readers who have a master-piece tucked away in the drawer of some agent's office in London, Paris or New York, to consider a summary of the history of *Waiting for Godot*. Written in about 1951, it first of all knocked around Paris, in the T.N.P. and elsewhere; then Roger Blin, having read it and decided to present it, was delayed a year, until January of 1953. After creating a critical sensation in Paris, it took another two and three-quarter years to reach the London stage. So if you have written a play and have sent it off to your agent or a management, forget about it and write a few more. They may come in handy for supplementing your old age pension!

In the event, of course, we benefited from having delayed our opening until after London. The play created an instant furore at the Arts. Almost without exception, the popular press dismissed it as obscure nonsense and pretentious rubbish. However, it was enthusiastically championed by Harold Hobson and Kenneth Tynan. As in Paris, it made the news columns of the daily papers, when indignant and respectable members of the community were moved to walk out of the theatre, or shout epithets at members of the cast. This sort of thing was by no means confined, of course, to London. In the Brussels production, a scandalized old lady stood up and shouted to her astonished companions in the stalls: 'Why don't they work?' Some wit in the upper part of the theatre, shouted back: 'Because they haven't time.'

In Dublin, the critical appraisal of the play was, as far as I can judge, more universally favourable than in any other city. This, I think, was partly due to the fact that, as I have mentioned before, the dialogue is more entertaining in Dublinese, so it is easier for the audience to enjoy the play, even though they may not appreciate its subtleties; and partly, dare I say it, because many of the Dublin critics were regular readers of the *Sunday Times* and the *Observer*. Of course, we didn't get off scot free. The *Evening Herald* said, 'Some of the grosser crudities, which were omitted or glossed over in London, were included here. They add nothing to the atmosphere, and are merely an attempt to out-Joyce the Joyce of *Ulysses*.'

We had, in fact, stuck to the original bargain with Sam, and played the play more or less exactly as he had translated it. In the London production, there had been a number of small cuts made by the Lord Chamberlain. After considerable pressure had been put on him, Sam reluctantly agreed to allow the play to be presented, omitting these passages and words; for he realized that, after such a long wait, there was not much point in cutting off his nose to spite his face. Unfortunately for the student of Beckett's plays, the text of the English publication is that of the stage production, and therefore is according to the Lord Chamberlain. For instance, on page seventeen, Estragon says: 'What about hanging ourselves?' In the English edition, the stage direction reads:

'Vladimir whispers to Estragon. Estragon highly excited.'

In the original, it reads:

ESTRAGON: What about hanging ourselves?
VLADIMIR: Hmm. It'd give us an erection.
ESTRAGON (*highly excited*): An erection!

78

I was very fortunate in my cast. The two tramps were played by Dermot Kelly and Austin Byrne, who had served me so well in *The Quare Fellow* the previous autumn; and the fruity voice of Nigel Fitzgerald, an Anglo-Irish actor who had toured for years with Anew MacMaster, brought a delightful relish to Pozzo's pomposities. Donal Donnelly was Lucky. He gave a magnificent performance, but the famous long speech was marred, I am afraid, by inadequate preparation. This was not Donal's fault. I had been most anxious to have him in the play, but he had contracted to play in Belfast during the greater part of our rehearsal period, and the only production I was able to give him before he left was five minutes in what surely must be the most unusual venue ever used for a theatrical rehearsal.

I cannot now recall the exact reason for this state of affairs, but we were unable to get together until a few minutes before his train left for the north, and the arrangement was that he should learn the speech during his period in Belfast. In order to give us the longest possible time at the job, we went into the toilet on the train, and went over the speech until the carriage was actually in motion, when I leapt out. I have always found that slow preparation in rehearsals is the only way for an actor to get full value out of the subtleties of a difficult part. Actors who have played a lot in repertory, tend to learn a part quickly—in some cases even before rehearsals have started. This has the effect of crystalizing any inadequacies in their own personal reading of the lines, and it is impossible for any producer to readjust the interpretation at a later stage. With a speech like Lucky's, which is words of gibberish, the sheer enormity of the task of memorizing made it imperative that the golden rule be broken. However, his mime was superb, and the intensity of feeling he brought to the slave's pathetic situation made it a landmark in his career and an event in the history of the Pike.

We acquired our Boy in Herbert Lane itself. I am sure the children of Herbert Lane who were between the ages of five and fourteen during this particular period must be the best educated of any in the world —from the point of view of European theatre at any rate. Our rehearsals have always been attended by anything up to half a dozen of them and they always listened with rapt attention to whatever we were rehearsing, from Ionesco to Christopher Fry. The only play that we did not permit these small drama students to attend was *Men without Shadows*, the torture sequences of which we felt to be unsuitable even for such sophisticated small ears. In this case our care for their susceptibilities was, I think, justified. Due to an oversight, the young daughter of an actress slipped in to the theatre during the rehearsal of a particularly brutal moment in the play. She had watched for ten minutes or so before I noticed her and had her sent away. Some nights later, her mother came quietly into the child's room to observe with horror the child beating her bound doll viciously across the face, snarling as she did so, 'Don't look at me, bastard!', which I regret to say is a direct quotation from M. Sartre.

So, anyway, we had no difficulty in getting a boy. It was just a question of which boy, and our choice fell in the end on Seamus Fitzgerald, who lived about five doors up, opposite the theatre. His performance was quite good, although he proved to be rather a thorn in the flesh to some of the cast, particularly Dermot Kelly—a natural 'Uncle Pether', and inclined to be a little irascible with the young, especially when asked the same set of questions in the confinement of an eight feet by four dressing-room, nightly over a period of six months.

What with the English papers, which are available in Ireland in Irish editions printed in Manchester (or, in the case of the grander ones, undiluted, so to speak) still full of controversy about the play's run in London, and the excellent notices we got in the Dublin papers, the play seemed set for a long run. The Pike was at last becoming an economic proposition. Our only outgoings were some pocket-money for the boy, and a modest emolument for a young stage manageress, the box-office rent, advertising, electricity, and the small overheads such as ground rent and rates. Shareholders, that is to say, the four actors and myself, drew salaries, which, though small were at least mentionable.

As the run progressed, various problems of an unusual nature presented themselves. First of all, there was the supply of bowler hats. Both tramps wear bowler hats, and at one point, a bowler hat is jumped on and generally maltreated as part of the action of the play. So we had to comb the Dublin second-hand clothes shops to satisfy the steady demand. Another problem was chicken. In Act One, Pozzo eats a portion of chicken in front of the hungry eyes of Vladimir and Estragon, and subsequently presents Estragon with the bones. In the small confines of our auditorium, there was no possibility of faking, so the families of those connected with the management of the theatre had a constant supply of chicken soup—a by-product of the property department—for as long as the run continued. However, occasionally some slip up would occur, and the stage manager would have to rush to the nearest hotel and beg an astonished manager for a leg of chicken 'to take away'.

There is something about the title of the play which captures the public imagination and in Dublin, even to a greater extent than in other cities, *Godot* became a catch-phrase. If anyone, from Jimmy O'Dea in the Gaiety Pantomime to a corner-boy propping up a betting office in one of the poorer quarters of the city, was asked for what they were waiting, the inevitable reply would come back, 'I'm waiting for Godda'. At the same time, there had been a lot of controversy about Henry Moore's reclining figure, and the *Irish Times* cartoonist 'N.O'K,' captioned a cartoon of a Civic Guard eyeing a tramp recumbent against a tree, reporting to his superior, 'I'm afraid it's going to be no run of the mill vagrancy case, he claims he's the Reclining Figure waiting for Godot.'

The phrase crept into journalistic usage over all sorts of irrelevant subjects. A letter in a daily paper, headed 'Idle Youth', read:

'Sir. Your columnist, Aknefton, was in extraordinary mood in your issue of November 19th. His column was headed "Idle Youth waiting for Godot". As his story unfolded, he was referring to corner boys, as he described them, loafing outside public houses and betting offices.

'That description would be more appropriate for another kind to be found lounging in the coffee-houses and lounge bars around Grafton Street, St. Stephen's Green and Baggot Street. They are the people waiting for "Godot". They have no problem as to where the next meal or night's shelter is to come from. It is they who have the time and money to bother about and discuss for hours the inane, purposeless philosophy of "Godot". Not so the young persons that Aknefton saw loafing at public houses and betting offices. They are the "Unemployable" and they "deserve censure" said "Aknefton". One would imagine we had employers crying out for idle, youthful hands. . . .'

The more serious writers, too, couldn't let the subject drop. Profiles of Beckett were published in the glossy monthlies. The Irish poet, Patrick Kavanagh, contributed a newspaper article entitled 'Some Reflections on *Waiting for Godot*', and Vivien Mercier reviewed the Faber publication. All this was unsolicited. The Public Relations Department of the Pike hadn't to resort to any of the stunts normally in the repertoire of a theatre publicist.

Early in December, my wife and I were touched to receive an invitation from Donald Albery to a sumptuous party, which he gave to celebrate the hundredth performance of the play in the Criterion. I was pleased to meet three other Godot producers among the guests—Peter Hall, Michael Myerberg, who was to present the play in America, and the producer of a projected Israeli presentation. During the course of the evening we were introduced to Sir Bronson Albery.

'Is Beckett coming to Dublin to see your show?' he asked.

I had regretfully to inform him that the author hadn't any very great wish to visit his native city, except for urgent family matters and so forth, and that I was afraid that he wouldn't be coming to see us.

'Uh,' chuckled Sir Bronson, 'don't suppose he'd even make the fare on your royalties!'

In the event, we had the last laugh on Sir Bronson, for when the final figures of the run in the Pike, Gate, a provincial tour, and a Dun Laoghaire production were totted up, the author's royalties exceeded what would have been possible for an English tour of the play, on a brief visit to one of Dublin's larger theatres. If Sir Bronson's company had come to Dublin I would not have put on the play in the Pike or elsewhere.

Incidentally, it was just after this party that Harold Hobson re-entered the ring, at about Round Ten of the *Godot* Contest. This time, with one of his rare bursts of acerbity, he wrote:

'Some time ago I remarked that Mr. Samuel Beckett's *Waiting for Godot* at the Criterion, besides being the loveliest, saddest, most haunting lyric, the most glorious threnody for hope deceiving, on the contemporary stage, was also one of the four funniest entertainments in London. That extremely naughty Bad Fairy, Mr. Malcom Muggeridge, whose swashbuckling suavity can sometimes charm, jeered at this observation, adding on a television programme that I must been thinking of *Titus Andronicus*.

'What happened then? Mr. Muggeridge associated himself with a piece which *he* thought funny, *The Punch Revue*, and I was mightily interested when it was booed on the first night, and withdrawn after a disappointing hobble. *Waiting for Godot* on the other hand, continues to run, and on Thursday celebrated its hundredth performance.'

This little outburst helped to keep the till clinking,

both in Piccadilly Circus and Herbert Lane, and also to counteract the pre-Christmas falling off, which is a feature of box-office the world over.

Now, alas, Donal had to leave us, largely because of a previously contracted Christmas show in another theatre, but also because he was in fact finding this part quite a strain, and had developed nasty abrasions on his neck from the constant rubbing of the rope by which Pozzo controlled his unfortunate servant. For a second-round Lucky, I was fortunate in securing Chris MacMaster, Anew MacMaster's son, who is now a television director for Granada. With the advantage of more orthodox rehearsal, he gave a better interpretation of the speech, but his mime never came quite up to the high standard set by his predecessor.

Godot seemed so set in its run by this time that we ventured the very unusual expedient for Dublin of presenting another production at a different theatre, while leaving *Godot* running in the Pike. This was a burlesque version of the old favourite, *Peg o' My Heart*, set in 1920 costume and specially designed to suit the Christmas trade. All this activity gave us a great sense of achievement and self-importance, that we have never quite recaptured. In several Dublin papers, as is I dare say the custom elsewhere, around New Year the theatre columnists publish lists of the high-lights of the preceding twelve months, which my wife and I always referred to as the End-of-Term Report. That year, we won the 'Best Play by Irish Author' stakes in the *Evening Herald*, despite what their critic Mr. Finegan had said about its 'grosser crudities'.

At the end of February, we released Nigel Fitzgerald for a couple of weeks, to play a highly-paid lead in the Olympia, and Fred Johnson, the ex-Abbey actor who now lives and works in London and who fortunately for us was visiting Dublin at the time, took over the part in Nigel's absence. Fred's interpretation was interesting, as his appearance and demeanour prompted me to allow him to play it more as the part had been played in France—that is to say, coarser and more *nouveau riche* than the gentlemanly Fitzgerald interpretation. I hope Fred will forgive me for putting it this way, but I expect he will know what I mean. After his two weeks' absence, Nigel rejoined us from *Love in a Mist*. I thought he seemed glad to be back.

By this time, we were hard at work on plans for a tour. Business had dropped off a little and, although I have no doubt that we could have continued to run without a further dropping off for a very long time indeed, had it been worth our while. But in the Pike, anything short of capacity is not enough to keep the shares at a level acceptable even in an 'art' theatre. We consequently decided to go out in a blaze of glory, and to move to the Gate Theatre before we set out over the mountains and bogs of Ireland. A number of people dislike visiting a back lane, particularly after having gone through the mumbo-jumbo of club membership, and then having to sit on hard benches with a minimum of sponge rubber to supplement their natural resources. We felt that a short run in a more conventional theatre would use up the remaining potential audience at our disposal. We were, if anything, pessimistic in our assessment, for the Gate broke its existing box-office records and I have no doubt that, had the theatre been available for a further period, we could have extended our run even longer.

During the last month or so in the Pike, we had been working very hard booking our tour. There are only four provincial theatres in Ireland, properly equipped for a visit from a professional company: Wexford, Waterford, Limerick and Clonmel. There used to be an excellent theatre in Cork, which was visited regularly by Dublin and cross-channel companies, as well as having local repertory seasons, but that was burnt down some years ago. Wexford has an excellent little theatre, which has been refurbished to suit the demands of their celebrated festival but, unfortunately, it was already booked for the period of our tour. The Corporation of Waterford has now refurnished and equipped its charming old municipal theatre, but at the time of which I am writing it was closed, pending these alterations. There was, however, a small civic theatre, normally used by the local amateur company.

There are no touring circuits, such as those which remain in truncated form in post-television England. People like Anew MacMaster and his indomitable wife, Margery (Micheál MacLiammoir's sister), know every inch of the territory, and play in halls throughout the length and breadth of the countryside. They have thirty years' or so experience of the business and know all the foibles of every town and village hall in the land. For instance, they know that you can never play Ballysomewhere on a certain week in March, because the County Drama Festival is held in another town, and you would get no audience. They know that the parish priest in Ballysomewhere else is an old skinflint and looks for so much rent for the hall that it is not worth visiting the town. Likewise, the curate in another place is a drama fan and will see to it that if you do bad business, the rent is waived.

We had none of this knowledge, so we decided that the only thing to do was to keep the tour as simple as possible. We would close in the Gate on the Saturday, do a week in north Leinster, where we would visit Dundalk, Navan and Drogheda, returning to Dublin for Holy Week, which is a traditional 'week out' in the Irish theatre; then open for Easter in Cork. We would play there for a week, and then visit Clonmel, Waterford and Carlow for a couple of days each. In the course of discussion about possible dates for the tour, Saint Patrick's College, Maynooth, where the majority of Irish Catholic clergy are trained, was suggested as a possible venue. A friend approached a member of the staff with whom he was acquainted, but was told that: '. . . the President (he controls such matters) after consideration decided that *Godot* would be theatrically too sophisticated for many of our students. He declined the offer with regret.' However, Maynooth is only twenty-odd miles from Navan, and a large number of the staff and students came over to see the production in that town. I must say, they made one of the best audiences we had played to. Incidentally, such are the complexities of ecclesiastical regulations that, while in the diocese of Meath, which included Dundalk, Drogheda and Navan, we operated under the blessing of the Administrator of the Diocese, which allowed clergy publicly to visit the performances. This is not the case in many dioceses, including Dublin and in order to advertise this fact, our posters were inscribed 'Con Permisu Ordinarii'.

We set off from the Gate to Dundalk in my Hill-man Husky, which had been equipped with a roof rack. Inside the vehicle, I was at the wheel, and there were all our spotlights, costumes and the calico tabs and legs which I had painted with a green, brown and black colour scheme similar to the original décor in the Pike. There was also Nigel Fitzgerald, his daughter, Nicky, who was our touring stage manager, and Gilbert McIntyre, who was our touring Lucky-cum-electrician. On the roof was the switchboard, various bits and pieces, including the mechanism for operating the 'moon', and to crown all, our mascot and essential property, 'a Tree'. Ahead of us had gone Austin Byrne, my wife, and our touring Boy, Ray Whelan, in Dermot Kelly's car. The reason for their earlier departure was that Dermot's vehicle was a vintage Morris, whose maximum speed was twenty-five miles per hour.

In Dundalk, we played the Dominican Hall, an excellently equipped theatre. I was told in that town that the prior, a theatrically-minded and progressive man, had no sooner built this fine theatre than he was shifted to Newry, where he immediately set about the same task. I have always been haunted by the vision of this indomitable priest, patiently moving from one town to another from Donegal to Cork, leaving a trail of theatres behind him. His reward will have to be in Heaven, for he will certainly not get it in the Land of Saints and Scholars.

In Navan, apart from the clerical enthusiasm mentioned above, there was one audience reaction remark which I feel should be recorded. Two old country-men were overheard discussing the play as they left the hall. 'What do they be sayin' at all?' asked one. 'I don't know,' said the other, 'I believe they do make it up as they go along.'

We had been warned by Anew McMaster of the inherent dangers of the town of Drogheda. Apart from a cinema, the rent of which was altogether too high for our purposes, the only possible venue was a rather gloomy Victorian hall, owned by inadequately financed trustees, who had been charged to operate it in the public interest. 'The public interest' didn't run to a sufficient supply of fuel for the boiler, or chairs, and these had to be specially bought and hired respectively for the occasion. The acoustics, too, were very echoey. I got round this by hiring rick covers from a firm of tent-makers in Dublin, which I laid on the floor as 'carpet' and hung from the front of the gallery to operate in the same way as the soft, cellular plaster in the back wall of a cinema. The warnings of both Mac and Lord Longford, who had had a disas-trous visit there some years before, had spurred us on to make this extra effort to break the jinx on this sad building. Our industry was amply rewarded, for we had the biggest audiences of our whole tour during the two nights we played there, and the low rent made it the most profitable date, despite the addi-tional expenses incurred.

Military duties made it impossible for me to accom-pany the production on its southern circuit. I had been in advance to Cork and Carlow to arrange about the bookings for halls there. Waterford and Clonmel had been arranged by post, as they were both well-known to various people connected with the company. Since the disastrous burning of the Cork Opera House, there has been no proper theatre in this city, though nowadays the reasonably large and well-equipped Father Matthew Hall is available. We went to the Catholic Young Men's Society Hall, which is small but was all that we could get, under the circumstances. It has an extraordinary proscenium arch, constructed in plywood in the form of a medieval castle, with latticed loopholes that light up at the touch of a switch. Needless to say, we did not touch the switch!

So the company set off on Easter Eve by train and I followed the subsequent week-end. They had a very good week and appreciative audiences, who, I was told enjoyed the play despite its peculiar frame. The distance from base of the Munster route made it necessary for a larger vehicle to be used and I hired a Commer station wagon from a small Drive Yourself Dublin motor company. They let me down rather badly, for on the trip down, the cylinder head cracked, and had to be patched up in a local garage. Worse was to befall. I returned by train on Sunday, as I had to be back first thing on Monday morning, and the company and my wife Carol set off for Clonmel. Half-way to Clonmel, the Commer blew two tyres. Disaster stared them in the face. However, they were able to thumb a lift for themselves and their equipment in a turf lorry. They arrived very late and very bedraggled, as they had travelled on top of the turf, sheltered from the lashing rain by sacking. To complete their misery, the amplifying equipment for incidental music gave up the ghost.

They were told in the theatre that the only man available on a Sunday who knew anything about this kind of equipment was Brendan Long who, as well as being a moving spirit in the local amateur movement, was also on the staff of the Clonmel paper, the *Munster Tribune*. Carol was sent out in search of him and ran him to earth, playing his Sunday game of golf. He immediately broke off his game and hurried to the theatre, where he took off his coat and started to work on repairing the faulty apparatus. Thus, five minutes before the advertised time of curtain rise, Clonmel's leading drama critic, as he turned out to be, was feverishly working on the wrong side of the proscenium. That he gave us an excellent notice was a tribute to his generosity of spirit.

To round off the tour, we had arranged for a return visit to County Dublin, where we played the Gas Company Theatre, Dun Laoghaire, and where Donal Donnelly rejoined us, as Gilbert McIntyre was committed to another engagement. Thus, during the adventures of *Godot* in Ireland, we had had five Luckys. Apart from those mentioned, the intervening ones had been Brendan Matthews and John Corish, who were both very good. Gilbert, despite his duties at the switchboard and unsuitable physique (he is tall, handsome and well built), was an extremely good Lucky. Of course, by this time, I had become the most experienced Lucky-producer in the business, and was able to give him the benefit of my practice on his predecessors.

Near the end of Act Two of *Waiting for Godot*, the following passage occurs:

'Lucky puts everything down, puts end of rope into Pozzo's hand, takes up everything again.
VLADIMIR: What is there in the bag?
POZZO: Sand. (*He jerks the rope.*) On.'

On the last night of the Dun Laoghaire date, our manager, Tom Willoughby, came through the foyer among the gas cookers, carrying a large suitcase.

'What's in the bag?' I asked casually.
'Gold,' said Tom.

Once more we had played to capacity business, so it seemed for once the prophet was not without honour in his own land.

I wonder all the same if, like the Abbey and *The Quare Fellow*, business would have been quite so brisk without the publicity accruing from the Paris and London productions. This question of publicity is an interesting one. While I know that a lot of worthless but skilfully publicized theatres *does* attract a large attendance and I firmly believe that a really good play well-produced will always attract a discriminating audience, I have become convinced that, to do outstanding business, both merit *and* publicity are necessary. Certainly, the antics of the inebriated Brendan, and the intellectual furore caused wherever *Godot* has been performed, seem in every case to have turned an artistic and reasonable success into a smash hit.

In America, however, the play doesn't appear to have had a triumph comparable with its impact in Europe, considering the potential of that vast country. Nevertheless, it was constantly in the news columns, and as any public relations officer will tell you, a few lines among the hard news is worth several columns on the theatre page. I quote from the *New York Herald Tribune* of the 23rd January 1957:

'The returned presentation of *Waiting for Godot*, the Samuel Beckett brain-teaser play that reopened at the Ethel Barrymore Theatre, Monday night, was shot down last night when the show's five stagehands refused to raise the curtain. Producer, Michael Myerberg said, that the stagehands, members of the International Alliance of Theatrical Stage Employees, presented a late afternoon demand to add two men to the backstage crew. When he refused, the crew refused to raise the curtain.

' "The show actually requires only one stagehand," he said, "but we originally hired five." The play was first presented last April at the John Golden Theatre and ran two months.

' "If five men were enough then, they are enough now," Mr. Myerberg said. He said that he would seek a court order today, and that the play would go on again tonight.

'There was no comment available from the stagehands' union.'

I was glad to note from this, that Broadway producers have their problems, too, though they seem a little different from our own.

Actually, the American production had a rough passage from the start. Sam wrote to me on 20th November 1955:

'The producer is Michael Myerberg and he plans, I am told, to open in Miami, of all ridiculous places, on Jan. 3rd and thence proceed by stages (c'est le cas de le dire) to N.Y. where opening is scheduled for Jan. 22nd approx.'

He again wrote on January 6th:

'. . . News from London continues good. But the Miami nobs and their critics seem displeased. No details as yet.'

94

Estragon and Vladimir were played by two famous American comics, Bert Lahr and Tom Ewell respectively. The production director was Alan Schneider, a sincere and sensitive man ideally suited to the job. Unfortunately, Lahr, who was a vaudeville man to his finger-tips, was not, to put it mildly, quite attuned to the subtleties of the play. He felt that he was the major star and the role of Estragon should be somewhat blown up in order to allow him to outshine Mr. Ewell. Mind you, Mr. Lahr is no eccentric in this attitude. As a matter of fact, the public would be amazed how frequently the emphasis of a script is twisted to meet the demands of their favourites. However, Mr. Schneider is not a man to sacrifice his principles to expediency, and he resigned from the enterprise before it reached New York. In that city, while it attracted considerable interest among intellectual circles (who, I may say, on the whole are very much more in touch with continental theatre than their English opposite numbers), it did not get the long run it deserved in the first instance. It was later re-produced, with an all-negro cast, in what I hear was a very interesting presentation.

After our enormous (for Dublin) success with *Waiting for Godot*, we were naturally anxious to get the first production of the author's next work, and the projected 1957 Dublin International Theatre Festival seemed to offer an opportunity. He had written another play, *Fin de Partie* but, unfortunately, his translation would not be completed in time for us. So we decided to give a reading of his radio play, *All that Fall*, in company with a mime he had devised for dancer, Derek Mendel, to do in Paris, for which

Sam's cousin, John Beckett, had composed music. Again we were unlucky, for John was unable to come to Dublin at the particular time required, to make the necessary adjustments to the score. Unlucky, is perhaps an understatement, for without a Beckett play to our hands, we decided to give for the festival the European *première* of a play by Tennessee Williams, called *The Rose Tattoo*.

A theatre could not be found for *Fin de Partie* in Paris, and its first production, by Roger Blin, was given in French at the Royal Court Theatre in London. This, I believe, infuriated French critical circles, who are very proud of their city's dominance in the world of intellectual theatre. Incidentally, I think their attitude in this respect possibly explains their recent panning of the superb Pinter play, *The Caretaker* which, in a general way, I suppose, could be said to be in the Beckett tradition; although I personally think it is a pity that he has had to fall back on the device of madness to 'explain' the situation and behaviour of one of its characters.

Fin de Partie was subsequently presented in English at the Royal Court Theatre under the title of *End Game*. There was a long delay before its production, due to the fact that the Lord Chamberlain wished the eradication of a longish passage, which he considered blasphemous. It appeared that, just as *The Hostage* had been acceptable in Dublin in Irish, but criticized for blasphemy in English, so his lordship did not object to what he considered blasphemy in French, for there had been no talk of cuts for the earlier Roger Blin production.

After a furore which arose in Dublin over the

second projected International Theatre Festival, when the Archbishop, Dr. McQuaid, was involved (I suspect unwittingly and unwillingly) in the rejection of a proposed presentation of Alan McClelland's dramatization of a portion of Joyce's *Ulysses* under the title of *Bloomsday*, Beckett refused to allow any of his work to be presented in Dublin. Being very anxious to give the first presentation of *End Game*, I asked the author if he would allow me to do the play in Belfast, which is outside the jurisdiction of the Lord Chamberlain and Dr. McQuaid alike. This he agreed to, subject to the Royal Court's approval but, sad to say (from our point of view), the Lord Chamberlain climbed down before the necessary arrangements could be made at our end and the play had its first English language production in Sloane Square, together with *Krapp's Last Tape*, which the author wrote especially for the Irish actor, Pat McGee. Apart from its merits as a piece of dramatic writing, it is interesting in that it is the first stage play of Beckett's to be written in the English language. It also has much more in common with his novels than his previous work for the stage. Cyril Cusack appeared in it when, together with *Arms and the Man*, he presented it as the Irish contribution to the Paris International Theatre Festival at the Sarah-Bernhardt Theatre.

The play on which Beckett is currently working, *Happy Days*, will also be in the English language, and will, I hope, have been presented by the time this book appears.

Chapter IV

PRODUCING
BECKETT AND BEHAN

~~~~~~

> A hungry feeling came o'er me stealing
> And the mice were squealing in my prison cell,
> And that old triangle
> Went jingle jangle,
> Along the banks of the Royal Canal.
> > *The curtain rises*
> The scene is the bottom floor or landing of a
> wing in a city prison. . . .

THE RECORDED VOICE of the author singing this song set the atmosphere for the first production of *The Quare Fellow*. I have already said that for a certain type of play, the most important consideration for the producer is to achieve the atmosphere. He has a number of resources available for this. First of all, there is the cast.

While every actor should be well trained and versatile, there are frequently cases when appearance and personality count for more than his purely professional qualifications. To assist in giving the production the right atmosphere it may well be worth the producer's while to devote time to schooling an inexperienced actor with the right characteristics. This will leave him less time for other members of the cast, but if he has seasoned actors, who are carefully chosen for the other parts, he can allow them to make their own way with help only in a general fashion. His judgement in this as to the relative importance of time spent on one actor or another, together with the initial choice of casting, is one of the first factors which, before rehearsals have begun, will make or mar the atmosphere and ultimately the production.

While on the subject of casting, however, it is interesting to note that Irish actors seem particularly suited to French plays, and I was very satisfied with the atmosphere achieved in two Sartre productions, *Nekrassov* and *Men without Shadows*. Translations from the French seem to flow very easily with Irish accents. In English, the public school and Establishment implications of a certain type of accent make it essential for the director to decide, when casting, exactly what social background a character comes from. In French or other contiental plays, this isn't always apparent from a reading of the script, and the characterization may be completely warped from the author's original intention if it is made clear, by the actor's accent, exactly what his father was. In Ireland (except among the pukka Anglo-Irish, who from Norman times have tended to marry upper-class English wives and vice versa, and have always had close ties with the British Army and Civil Service) accents are regional and not social. It is therefore much more difficult to pin down a person's 'status' from their way of speech.

The other resources available to the producer for the purpose of establishing his atmosphere are setting, lighting, and sound effects. One thing particularly

evocative of the interior of a prison building is the
hollow echo. Even to those who haven't first-hand
experience of such places it must be obvious that a
large stone building, without carpets or soft furnish-
ings of any kind, fitted throughout with steel doors
and iron staircases, must magnify the smallest sound.
So I got my P.R.O., Steve (Rosamund Stevens), who
is a resourceful lady, capable of fulfilling the most
difficult and improbable assignments, to capture
Brendan, suitably lubricate his vocal chords, and
transport him, together with a recording engineer
and his equipment, to a large empty hall to record
this song. This difficult task she accomplished superbly.
Unfortunately the recording, which was one of the
best I have ever heard of the author singing that particular ballad, was lent to my friend, the late Sean
Mooney, stage manager of the Abbey, whose tragic
death occurred before I had a chance to get it back
from him, and it is lost to posterity. Brendan's rich
North City voice resonantly recorded, representing
the voice of a prisoner confined in 'chokey' (a punish-
ment cell), followed by and mingling with the clank
of keys and the rattle of bolts as Warder Donnelly
opened up the cells on his morning rounds gave the
most law-abiding members of the audience a sinking
feeling of claustrophobia, even before the lights crept
on to reveal the five cell doors which are the only
essentials for the setting of Act One. Naturally
enough the effect on those who had been 'inside' (of
whom our audiences numbered not a few!) was still
more potent.

The size and resources of the Pike obviously made
it impossible to give anything approaching a realistic

representation of a prison landing; but having seen
the Abbey and television productions of the play,
where greater realism was obtained, I believe that the
atmosphere of claustrophobia and isolation, which are
the basic ingredients of prison life, were better expressed by our five white door frames, constructed in
perspective and holding plain black numbered doors.
Actually, in reality, the interior of prisons tend to be
whitewashed or stone, and are generally quite
brightly lit during daylight hours by the glass roof
that usually illuminates each wing. But practical con-
siderations in the Pike, which always have to be
aimed at concealing the minute size of the acting
area, made a dimmer and more concentrated light a
necessity. This again helped to emphasize the division
between the prisoners and the outside world although
in fact, its intensity bore little relation to the truth.

In *Waiting for Godot* the objective of the producer
should be to create the feeling that these four characters are isolated in Eternity. During the run in the
Pike, members of the audience often commented on
the suitability of the tiny stage for the play. I don't
agree with this at all. I think the ideal setting for this
cosmic piece is on a huge stage where, in a little pool
of light, Vladimir and Estragon, Pozzo and Lucky,
perform their antics around the tree. The vast empti-
ness about them would serve to emphasize their de-
pendence on one another and their isolation within
the enormity of the universe. By the time this book is
published, the play will have received such a production in Paris. The grandeur and simplicity of *Waiting
for Godot* is surely no better expressed than in the
stage directions for Act One:

> A country road. A tree.
> Evening.

The atmosphere of *End Game* is more specific, and does not leave so much to the imagination of the producer and designer.

> Bare interior.
> Grey light.
> Left and right back, high up, two small windows, curtains drawn.
> Front right, a door. Hanging near door, its face to wall, a picture.
> Front left, touching each other, covered with an old sheet, two ashbins.
> Centre, in an armchair on castors, covered with an old sheet, Hamm.
> Motionless by the door, his eyes fixed on Hamm, Clov. Very red face.

Krapp's Den must suggest decayed suburban late Victoriana or Edwardiana, not unlike the effect achieved by Donald McWhinney and his designer in *The Caretaker*, though perhaps with a hint of the slightly more absolute feeling of Ranelagh in Dublin.

As radio plays, *Embers* and *All that Fall*, being in a completely different idiom, don't present the same problems of creation of atmosphere as arise in a stage play. But the author, as always, is tersely specific, and if his directions are followed precisely, as they were by Mr. McWhinney, the imagination of the unseen audience should do the rest. What could be more straightforward than . . .

> Sea scarcely audible.
> HENRY's boots on shingle. He halts.
> Sea a little louder.

which are the opening directions of *Embers*?

If the authentic atmosphere of *The Quare Fellow* is all important, that of *The Hostage* is not. In the London production, Miss Joan Littlewood gave to the play something of her own personality and the robust Cockney fervour which is so much a part and parcel of Stratford East. This mingled admirably with the ribald, irreverent inconsequence of Brendan's script, and made it hugely acceptable to an English audience completely ignorant of the whys and wherefores of Irish politics.

When the play visited Dublin on tour, concessions were made to Irish ears by the recasting of certain parts with well-known Dublin actors like Dermot Kelly, but although the play did enormous business at the box-office, the offence it caused in certain quarters was not entirely due to the religious susceptibilities of many of the audience, but was in part engendered by the alien approach of the direction. Miss Littlewood's production re-created by Miss Avis Bunnage for touring, although superb artistically and technically, was just not 'Irish' enough for a Dublin audience.

In addition to *The Quare Fellow* and *The Hostage*, Brendan has written a radio play (which was done for the B.B.C.) and two radio sketches which were performed some years ago on Radio Eireann. The two Radio Eireann pieces, *The Garden Party* and *The New House* are, like *The Quare Fellow* more or less complete anecdotage. They are, in fact, humorous and indeed farcical developments of two incidents during and shortly after the move of the Behan family from a North City slum to their previously mentioned residence in Kildare Road.

The New House describes the resentment of Stephen when the benevolence of the Dublin Corporation transplanted him away from his neighbours, his work, and the various licensed premises around the immediate neighbourhood of the tenement which had so long been his home, to the arid concrete wastes of distant Crumlin. Kathleen, with a mother's natural wish to bring up her children in a more healthy atmosphere, and her understandable desire to ease her own working conditions by the acquisition of a proper kitchen, bathroom, garden, and other amenities, felt quite differently. Stephen employed every delaying tactic he could devise to prevent the move, but ultimately his wife took matters into her own hands, and he returned home one evening to find a curt note to the effect that his tea would be served at 77 Kildare Road. His adventures *en route*, culminating in his alcoholic arrival in the small hours, are uproariously depicted in the sketch. Dominic also describes the incident in his autobiography *Teems of Times and Happy Returns*.

The companion piece, with equal hilarity, relates Kathleen's efforts to get the garden dug, and the preposterous devices used by her husband to avoid having to lay his own hand to a spade. I may say that to this day the garden does its best to return to that state of rural exuberance from which the corporation bulldozers so rudely tore it.

The Big House, though no doubt based on an actual incident related to Brendan over a pint, is at the same time more imaginative and thoughtful, and contains a considerable amount of incisive social criticism concealed beneath its high comedy. As a piece of writing, it is more comparable to *The Hostage* than to his other work. Set during the Civil War in the early twenties, the characterization is in some instances that of the forties or fifties. This indicates a slapdash disregard for actualities also to be found in *The Hostage*. For instance, it is almost impossible to make out whether the author intends Miss Gilchrist to be a sort of lapsed Protestant Salvationist (Gilchrist is a North of Ireland name), or a backsliding functionary of the Legion of Mary. The line, 'I stand fast by my Lord and will sing my hymn now', would seem to have its origins in a revivalist hall in Ballymacarratt, Belfast. However, a couple of lines later on, Meg exhorts her to 'Get off the stage, you Castle Catholic bitch!'

Possibly, of course, Brendan intended it as a general jeer at the absurdities of the various religious lunatic fringes, in which case accuracy of characterization is hardly an issue. But I merely make the point in order to indicate the difference between his general approach to *The Big House* and *The Hostage* on the one hand, and *The Quare Fellow* on the other. In the latter piece, the characters are carefully observed, not too wildly exaggerated portraits of classical realism, and his development as a writer seems to parallel the work of a painter like Picasso, who moved from precise realism to the purely non-representational abstract.

This seems to be in fact a recurring pattern among writers. Tennessee Williams and Sean O'Casey are two well-known examples that come to my mind, though unlike these two, Brendan seems to have gained greater popularity by his move towards fantasy. I wonder what would have been the result if

Miss Joan Littlewood had had a hand in *The Bishop's Bonfire* or *Cock-a-doodle-Dandy*?

I missed *The Big House* when it was broadcast by the B.B.C., but Brendan allowed me to adapt it for the stage. At a first reading, this would appear to be an impossibility. The play switches rapidly from the bedroom of Mr. and Mrs. Baldcock, to the servant's quarters and passageways in the house, to the roof, to the front of a lorry, to a scrap yard, to a pub, to the back of the lorry, to a party, and to Holyhead railway station. I found that by using the sort of technique required by Thornton Wilder for *Our Town*, and by ignoring all the setting difficulties completely, the audience quite happily accepted the convention.

It is not a full-length play and I wanted to couple it with Sean O'Casey's *Hall of Healing* which would have made a very interesting double bill. Unfortunately, the restrictions placed by Mr. O'Casey on the presentation of his plays in Dublin since the 1958 Theatre Festival made this impossible, and instead we played it with *Men without Shadows*. After we had run the double bill for about a month, I felt that there were a lot of people who couldn't face the horrors of the Sartre, but who would be glad to see the Behan play; so I replaced *Men without Shadows* by the two farcical sketches mentioned above, under the general title of *The New House*. This proved to be a mistake, as it didn't make sufficient contrast and the combined Behan evening didn't have the appeal one might expect.

If Brendan's development as a writer towards the non-representational can be compared with more recent developments in pictorial art, Sam's play-writing puts one more in mind of a certain school of abstract sculpture. While Brendan attacks his canvas with great, carelessly applied strokes of emotion and humour, Sam, on the other hand, gives the feeling of the finely applied chisel and the precision of a master craftsman, as well as an artist. For me, at any rate, in his radio plays for instance, Beckett seems to evoke delicately a period of Irish life whose decay and ulti-mate disappearance was heralded by the complete gutting and refitting with polished glass, wrought-iron work and smooth upholstery of Davy Byrnes, in Duke Street.

Being the abstract writer he is, he doesn't go in for the precise images or detailed reminiscence of Joyce or O'Casey, but the line in *Embers*, 'Are you coming for a dip?' evokes for me with startling clarity bicycle trips with my own father to the Forty Foot, that all-male bathing place close to the Martello Tower at Sandycove, so well known to students of Joyce.

Because of emigration and the low marriage rate, there has been a tendency in Ireland for a number of years for the old and middle-aged to be more in evi-dence than in other countries. This I am convinced, though I am sure the author would not admit to it, has subconsciously affected Beckett's work. He would at all times have been apart from the robust, uninhibi-ted life of the new Dublin Corporation building schemes. It is this background that enabled Brendan to write the simple Boy Meets Girl episode of *The Hostage*. He, of course, is fully conversant with Leslie, Teresa's English counterpart, from his Borstal experi-ence. In fact, I can see that part of the attraction of

The Hostage was this little love story, which in its simplicity is comparable to the touching romance of the Negro sailor with the heroine of Shelagh Delaney's *A Taste of Honey*.

It is interesting to note that while a number of modern French writers such as Sartre express their philosophical theories by means of complicated emotional involvement of male and female, Beckett seems to avoid, superficially at any rate, anything of that sort. In fact, the only example of it in his playwriting for the stage is the twice repeated punt sequence in *Krapp's Last Tape*. This is very skilfully written and penetrating, and shows that he can well do it when he wants to. It will be remembered, however, that this is in narrative form and not in direct dialogue.

In the much talked of Lawrence Durrell *Alexandria Quartet*, the author explores, in four long novels, nearly every combination and permutation of human emotional entanglements. An interesting feature of *Waiting for Godot* is that although sex is not involved in any way, the relationship between Estragon and Vladimir is a sort of templet for all human emotional relationships. In fact, it is possible, if one knows the play well, to categorize all one's emotional relationships in terms of the two tramps. To one person, one is the Vladimir to their Estragon, to another, one is the Estragon to their Vladimir. It is not as simple as it sounds, because sometimes, under certain circumstances, one switches roles. My wife and I used to have an amusing sort of parlour game (which we used as a time-passer on long journeys) in which we would try to fit all our individual relationships with our close friends, parents and so forth, into this pattern. If you know the play well, try it sometime.

The Irish, like the Russians, are basically a peasant race, which may be a guide as to the apparent similarity between their respective relations with women. The fundamental moral monogamy, on which the teaching of both Catholic and Protestant Churches lays so much stress, is largely adhered to. The same stress on monogamy and an ordered family life is very strongly reflected in various Soviet pronouncements on such matters. In fact, the pontifications on Western decadence so frequently quoted by *Tass*, bear a marked resemblance to an Irish Diocesan Lenten Pastoral. There are those who hint darkly about the sex inhibitions caused by this teaching, at least as applied to Ireland, and suggest that this fidelity and so forth, is merely the lid pressing down on a seething mass of inhibitions and frustrations and that it is only the 'What would the neighbours think' restraint, natural to a small semi-rural community, that prevents a mass outbreak of the divorces, infidelities and sex abnormalities which seem to have become a feature of life in other Western countries.

The fact remains, however, that Beckett, Behan and indeed O'Casey (who is loudest of all in his condemnation of clerical repression of normal sex instincts) are monogamous and normal to a man. I am no Frank Harris, and do not propose to make a dramatic exposé of the sex lives of either of my subjects. But even if I did, I should have to make thorough investigation of their intimate experiences before I could attempt to do so. For two such unorthodox and convention-defying men, they both seem to have been conventionally and undramatically orthodox in their fidelity. Until Brendan brought Beatrice to the Pike I had never seen him with or heard of his 'dating' any member of the opposite sex. Likewise, although I don't know Sam as well as Brendan, Suzanne is the only name I have ever heard linked with his.

When Irishmen do get romantically involved, it seems to be in the messy, indecisive manner of the hero of Chekov's *Platanov,* and more than one demented foreigner has complained to me that, 'Basically you Irish prefer drink to women!' Certainly, except for occasional flashes, both Brendan and Sean O'Casey seems to have devoted their finest writing to descriptions of drinking:

'Will ya come down outa tha', some of yez one of yez will yez before I lay one o' yez out,'

as spoken by the drunken Fluther in the *Plough and the Stars,* is one of the author's epic lines, while the following quotation from Act I of *The Quare Fellow* will surely live in literary history as one of the most classic descriptions of a hang-over ever written:

NEIGHBOUR   Only then to wake up on some lobby and the hard floor boards under you, and a lump of hard filth for your pillow and the cold and the drink shaking you, and the dry retching to come on you, and wishing it was morning for the market pubs to open, where if you had the price of a glass of cider, you could sit down in the heat, anyway. Except, God look down on you, if it was a Sunday.

DUNLAVIN   Ah, there's the agony. No pub open, but the bells battering your bared nerves, and all you could do with the cold and the sickness was to lean over on your side, and wish that God would call you.

Any newspaper reader is thoroughly familiar with Brendan's alcoholic progress through public life, but the audiences who enjoy the finished product on the stages of London or New York may not be aware of the basic laziness which has to be overcome before the author can write even a short newspaper article. I myself am one of the laziest people I know—which makes me particularly sympathetic to Brendan's weakness. In my case, this may be due to the fact that, because my father got into financial difficulties, he took me away from school when I was only fifteen. Consequently I never learned the self-discipline and ordered concentration which should be the fruits of study in the higher forms of secondary school and are normally acquired before entering University. In fact, one of the reasons why theatrical production appeals to me as a profession is the rigid disciplines which are, willy-nilly, imposed on the director. There is an inexorable compulsion about the thought of twelve or more actors impatiently awaiting one's arrival at rehearsal which demands punctuality—and their dumb presence in front of one on the stage makes thought and action an absolute necessity. Brendan suffers from the same disability. He is very loyal to the excellent education provided by Her (or in those days His) Majesty's Borstal Institution, but I dare say the general upsets of youthful membership of an Illegal Organization not long after he completed his primary education, and the particular irritations of a longish period in adult remand prisons before settling down in Hollesley Bay, had the same effect on him as my own educational disadvantages had on me.

When he was a painter, the vital necessity of obtaining pint money compelled him to report to his foreman at 8 a.m.—because he knew that if he didn't clock in on time, his pay packet would be correspondingly thinner on Friday. As soon as the foreman's back was turned, of course, Brendan would be chatting away or, if feasible, slipping down to the nearest pub with a few of the boys—but this would hardly affect the emolument of anyone as capable as Brendan of providing an explanation if his absence was discovered.

Today, as a famous man of letters, the same simple logic motivates him, and the only way in which his natural resistance to work can be overcome is by an immediate need for money which can only be resolved by his turning in the goods. While his earliest efforts as a writer may have been produced purely for the joy of it, nowadays, notwithstanding his spontaneous generosity (such as the donation of his royalties from the stage production of *The Big House* to my Rose Tattoo Defence Fund) he is—and quite rightly so—implacably professional. Since the success of *The Quare Fellow*, which placed him in a Seller's Market, he has been a strictly C.O.D. man. In fact, all his work since that time has been actually commissioned. The editor of a Dublin 'glossy' told me that Brendan used to appear in the office with his piece in one hand and the other held out for the cheque. *The Big House* was commissioned by the B.B.C. Third Programme and *The Hostage* by Gael Linn—and *Vogue*, *The New Yorker* and other periodicals which are the El Dorado of most writers of his age, have queued up for any scraps let over from his typewriter.

Normally, of course, except for a modest advance, a playwright's royalties are paid in retrospect. He writes the play, receives his advance, and in due course the royalties start rolling in, proportionately to the success of the production. However, when revision is necessary, the rules of primitive economics go by the board. The author is expected to turn in work for no other reward than the assurance of the producer that such improvements as may be effected will increase the popularity of the play and thereby in three months' (six months', or two years') time, increase the money that the author may (in the opinion of the producer) ultimately receive. This is much too intangible a concept for a man brought up on the 'earn it-drink it-and then earn more' school. Joan Littlewood must have discovered this to her cost when getting him to do the necessary revisions for her London production of *The Hostage*. Having presumably paid him for his advance for the translation from the original Irish, she went away on a long holiday—so the story goes—leaving him ensconced in her flat with instructions to get the play into shape so that rehearsals could start immediately on her return. When she came back, she found no typescript—but a liberal supply of empty bottles. However, if rumour is correct, she then held him captive for a while, during which time the protesting Brendan dictated the necessary revisions—sometimes from the horizontal. I cannot vouch for the accuracy of this story, but there is no doubt that a simple perusal of his published work reveals the careless disregard for accuracy in characterization already referred to, and a constant re-use of phrases, gags and anecdotes which is part and parcel of a very proper dislike for work. For instance, the gag:

NEIGHBOUR   Many's the time the Bible was a consolation to a fellow all alone in the old cell. The lovely thin paper with a bit of mattress coir in it, if you could get a match or a bit of tinder or any class of light, was as good a smoke as ever I tasted.

is based on a presumably authentic remark he heard while in prison in England and is used in *Borstal Boy*.

The inability to get down to work until the wolf can be plainly heard scratching at the door has now become a major obstacle to Brendan's further output. As I write, I believe he has a portion of his new play in the rough, and not long ago Joan Littlewood travelled to Dublin with the idea of encouraging him to complete it. As far as I can make out, the only tangible result of her visit was to put him on the beer again. Brendan himself, I believe, attributes his alcoholic outburst to the refusal of Gael Linn to present a new Gaelic piece in its entirety. (After having seen the English version of *The Hostage*, the vigilantes are now on the *qui vive* for naughtiness 'through the medium of the language'.) Whatever the causes, he embarked on a gigantic batter culminating in the Dublin Dis-

11. Lucky's dance.

12. Serafina and Alvario.

trict Courts, and has been in and out of trouble in Canada and the U.S.A. ever since.

Brendan's happy-go-lucky, slapdash approach to his writing should, in the ordinary way, have prevented his work from ever being produced. *The Quare Fellow* breaks pretty well all the rules for good play-writing. It is rambling, without plot, and the principal serious character (Warder Regan) doesn't appear consistently throughout the play, which perhaps tempted Miss Littlewood to form the amalgamation with Donnelly mentioned in Chapter II. The two principal comedy characters, Dunlavin and Neighbour, don't appear at all in Act Three, although they are heard briefly as 'voices off'. Actually, in my Pike production, I slightly ameliorated this latter deficiency by having their cell windows visible to the audience. This was a wildly implausible departure from realism, but once the audience had accepted the twelve by twelve Pike stage as the exercise yard of Mountjoy Prison, they were ready for anything, and the fact that these characters appeared like Jack-in-the-boxes seven feet above stage level didn't seem to trouble them at all.

I seem to have spent the last page denigrating Brendan and enumerating all the reasons why his plays should not have been produced. The fact remains that I regard *The Quare Fellow* as the most moving and important Irish play since *The Plough and the Stars*. I felt this when I first read the play and I still feel it. I regard *The Hostage* as a very fine theatrical abstract which Miss Littlewood mounted and framed in such a way as to make it acceptable to a wide international audience that was neither interested by nor informed on the Irish political scene or 'ways of life'.

What qualities, therefore, are there in these plays to lift them from the disjointed jottings of an Irish drunk into the realms of greatness? The answer, I think, lies in Brendan's own personality. First of all there are his obvious selling points, such as his quick wit and the good-natured irreverence with which he approaches life; and, secondly, there is his immense and deep-seated affection for humanity as a whole, notwithstanding his very accurate observations of its shortcomings.

Of all the playwrights that I know about, with the exception of Jean Genet, he is the only one who, both in temperament and experience, is genuinely sympathetic with what goes on on both sides of the fence —and under it. His years in prison taught him that those whom society rejected are just human beings that have been found out, and that they have good and bad qualities precisely corresponding to their free brethren. 'For what's a crook, only a businessman without a shop,' as Prisoner A remarks at the end of Act Three of *The Quare Fellow*. On the other hand, his attractive personality has given him the entrée to circles in which he has met many orthodox, respectable and well-to-do citizens, and so he equally realizes that a bank balance is no greater guide to a human being's real merits or deficiencies than a prison record.

The only other playwright with whom he fully shares this universal humanity is Jean Genet. Genet, for instance, devotes his play *The Balcony* to the thesis that the paraphernalia of office makes the man, and if you dress a burglar as a judge, he will behave accordingly. In *The Blacks*, he points out, among other things, that to be black is no guarantee of excellence any more than to be white.

Brendan's background and early experience of English prison life have given him the edge even on Sean O'Casey, for although no one, least of all myself, could presume to question the old man's humanity, his Protestant upbringing and associations must have set him apart a little from his Catholic neighbours and workmates. Actually, Brendan is the first Irish Catholic to receive international recognition as a playwright, and also is one of the very few writers of repute with a genuinely working-class upbringing. Of course, the basic philosophy which enables Brendan to think and feel in this way does stem from his father, Stephen, and without it his prison experience might have just left him with a chip on his shoulder.

I think also that his rich humanity owes more to Roman Catholicism than is superficially apparent. Although he couldn't in the least be described as a model son of the Church, I believe that this great love of his fellow-men does originate in part, at least, from his Roman Catholic background. There is something about a Protestant upbringing, however vague, which seems to breed priggishness. With a Roman Catholic, the elaborate machinery of the confessional and the codification of sin gives the most heinous sinner the certainty that, having gone through the rigmarole of absolution and penance, he can walk down the aisle with his head held as high and with as firm a step as a nun who has confessed to a few minor infringements of the regulations of her order.

The Protestant tradition, on the other hand, with

its emphasis on the ultimate responsibility of the individual and the spurning of the impersonal formalities of forgiveness, such as intercessions to the saints, indulgences and so forth, tends to breed arrogance and self-satisfaction in those who feel that, through their own efforts, they are Saved, or 'right with God'. I am aware, of course, that this state of affairs is not the intention of Protestant teaching, but I believe that inadvertently it is the effect. Of course, the strange feature of Irish life is that among the middle and lower middle classes, Catholics and Protestants seem to have interchanged many of their less pleasant traits; thus a Protestant priggishness and self-satisfaction are frequently to be found among the Catholic *petit bourgoisie.*

I have described what I believe to be the basic causes of the immense love of humanity which shines through Brendan's dramatic writing. I don't know Sam Beckett as well as I know Brendan and I have no intimate knowledge of his family and background. True, in all my personal dealings with him I have found him very kindly and a short conversation with him, once his initial reserve has been penetrated, reveals a very gentle and good-natured disposition. Nevertheless, I am not in as favourable a position to analyse the causes for the compassion for humanity which is revealed in his work, and which makes a common bond between the two authors. Maybe he acquired it indirectly from the same sources as Brendan in Ireland, or maybe he was born with it. I couldn't say. Possibly he got some of it from his association with the Parisian Liberal philosophers with whom he mixed after leaving Dublin. Though

I doubt it, because the impression he gives me is of a person who has changed very little since he first left University. Anyway, it exists, as anyone of the slightest sensitivity who has seen or read the plays must be aware.

Waiting for Godot seems to have a laxative effect on critics. No play I have ever been involved with has produced such lengthy and intricate literary and dramatic expositions in the newspapers and periodicals as *Godot*. It was with a view to curtailing this spate of learned analysis, or rather its effects on the English public, that I was unwise enough to write a programme note for the revival of the play that I directed at Theatre Workshop recently. For I believe that the only possible approach to *Godot*, for director, actors and audience alike, is on a strictly emotional basis.

Sam has resolutely, over the years, refused to give any 'explanation' of his play. He is right in this, for how could you ask an artist to 'explain' an abstract picture, or how could you ask a poet to 'explain' a poem? However, in the case of a picture or a poem, the artist deals direct with the public, producer-consumer, as it were. In other words, the completed picture is seen by the purchaser exactly as it left the artist's studio. The middlemen (the gallery or organizers of the exhibition) merely arrange finance and display. They do not have any artistic function whatsoever. But with a play, there are at least two stages that the work of art must go through between the author's typewriter and the mind of a member of the audience. First of all, there is the producer, who has to think out how he is going to produce the play, and what is almost as important (if not more so), pick his cast. Then the actor, guided to a certain extent by the producer, speaks the lines and does the business—and more than likely adds something of his own personality to the original concept of the author, which has already been interpreted by the producer.

Finally, the member of the audience himself is affected by a number of factors, none of which have anything whatsoever to do with the playwright. First of all, there is the location of the theatre, and the price, if any, of his seats. Incidentally, I have often noticed that an invited audience is never as appreciative as a paying one. (I suppose this is due to a sort of instinctive feeling that something one gets for nothing isn't as good as something for which one has paid.) The location of the theatre can affect the customer in a number of different ways. If, for instance, he has come a long way to an obscure, out-of-the-way, uncomfortable art theatre like the Pike, he will be either determined to enjoy himself, having taken so much trouble to get there, or else resentful of all the inconvenience he has been put to, and approach the piece with a 'this had better be good or else' attitude. His relationship, also, with all the other members of the audience is very important. If, for instance, an Englishman with very little knowledge of Ireland comes to a theatre in Dublin, he may be infected by the enthusiasm of the rest of the audience, and enjoy a play, the subtleties of which are completely lost on him. On the other hand, he might see the same play performed by the same actors in England, surrounded by an audience consisting largely of people like himself, and not enjoy it at all. Sometimes a combination of these circumstances can have very unfortunate results. For instance, I have seen Irish plays performed in England with a mixed audience, consisting of one-third to a half of Irish ex-patriots, and the remainder English. When this happens, it seems that the laughter of the Irish members of the audience at points not understood or appreciated by the English contingent, far from aiding the enjoyment of the latter, merely irritates them.

I have found *Waiting for Godot*, not having a definite plot line and depending as it does on a rapport which must be set up between audience and actors, particularly susceptible to all the factors mentioned above. When I first received the script from Sam Beckett, early in 1954, my immediate reaction was that the two tramps should be played as two Dublin characters. On reading a play the first time through, I always tend to hear it in my mind's ear as I hope it will be played and in the case of *Godot* I have never had any doubts as to the correctness for me at any rate, of this first impression.

The play as originally written in French contained a lot of subtleties which are inevitably lost in the English language even when translated by the author himself. One of the most important, for instance, is the very opening line, which is, '*Rien à faire*'. Sam has translated this as, 'Nothing to be done.' Now this is obviously very important because, for the tramps, there *is* nothing to be done. But in French, this is a colloquialism, and can be thrown away with a sigh as just a little exclamation of tedium. In my original Dublin production I changed it to 'It's no good', be-

cause I felt that it was more colloquial and less significant. However, I subsequently discussed it with Sam,
and he was most emphatic that he wished it to be
spoken as 'Nothing to be done'. I still think that this
feeling should creep up on the audience unnoticably,
as it must do when spoken in French; but there seems
to be no possible English equivalent.

When I reproduced the play recently at Theatre
Workshop, some of the London critics attacked the
concept of using a Dublin dialect for the tramps.
Apart from my own personal feelings, there are other
good reasons for doing this when playing the play in
English. However, the personal feelings of the producer are very important, because if he has a particular conception of how the dialogue of any play should
be spoken, obviously he will get the best results from
following his own instincts. But there are more
general reasons why I think a Dublin dialect is helpful
to the fullest interpretation of the play.

When it was originally acted in French, the question of dialect didn't arise, because, by and large,
there was no reason why the tramps should not speak
perfect French. Accent in France is not a matter of
class or education, except in the extremes of provincial patois or Parisian argot. In his English translation, Sam has used a number of long or erudite
words, which would sound strange coming from the
mouth of a Cockney, or even a Liverpudlian. If it is
played with an Old Vic or Oxford accent, as Hugh
Burden played it in the Criterion Theatre, London,
one is immediately faced with the slight puzzlement
of how someone so erudite could become such a
scrofulous hobo. However, the Dubliner of humble

circumstance, like his Negro or Indian counterpart, tends to use longer words and more elegant syntax than his educational level would seem to warrant by English standards. Thus for instance the line:

'For the moment he's inert but he might run amuck any minute,' sounds plausible in a Dublin voice, while the word 'inert', coming from the mouth of an English tramp, would sound strange.

Dublin down-and-outs sometimes misuse long words, or use them in a slightly unusual way. So Vladimir's line:

'But it's not for nothing I've lived through this long day and I can assure you it's very near the end of its repertory,' although not in any way intrinsically Irish, flows very easily in the Dublin accent. There are, of course, throughout the play, a number of actual Dublinisms, such as Estragon's referring to Godot as 'your man' and Vladimir's 'I'd like well to hear him think,' but this sort of thing is not of such great importance as the general tenor of Vladimir's phraseology. Estragon, being a simpler and less voluble character, can be quite convincing in any dialect, as was proved by the playing of the part by Peter Woodthorpe in broad Yorkshire, in the original Criterion production.

One English critic said of my recent production, 'The language runs naturally into Irish cadences, but the trouble is that a good deal of it starts sounding like blarney.' To me, at any rate, this is a good thing, if by 'blarney' the critic means triviality. After all, Vladimir does remark in Act Two: 'This is becoming really insignificant.' How many human beings go around discussing life in a significant way? Very few,

I suspect, except perhaps in the more intense English plays, like those of John Whiting and Arnold Wesker.

'They give birth astride of a grave, the light gleams an instant, then it is night once more,' is Samuel Beckett's view of a human life, as expressed through the mouth of Pozzo. When you consider the insignificance of the greatest or most famous human being as against the enormity of time and the universe, surely our most profound philosophies are as 'blarney'?

My interpretation of the part of Pozzo is widely different from that of Roger Blin in France, and of any others I have heard about. The general reading of this character seems to be of an overbearing, bullying tycoon. Because of my own Irishness, however, I see him as an Anglo-Irish or English gentleman, whose excellent manners and superficially elaborate concern for others conceals an arrogant and selfish nature. The English upper classes are frequently horrified by the brutal treatment meted out by the other white races to their black or brown colonial possessions. But I believe that their own calm, almost unconscious assumption of superiority hurts and distresses these people even more than the downright bullying of others.

To me, the key to Pozzo's character is:

POZZO Leave him in peace. Can't you see he wants to rest? Basket! (*He strikes a match and begins to light his pipe . . . As Lucky does not move Pozzo throws the match angrily away and jerks the rope.*) Basket!

I therefore cast Nigel Fitzgerald who, although, as he frequently points out, is completely Irish, was in the

British Army during the war and has a rich, fruity *Anglo*-Irish voice, which he probably acquired at his English public school. The relationship established between the tramps and Pozzo is thus comparable to that between the native Irish and an Anglo-Irish or English landowner. This may or may not have been what Sam Beckett intended, but it certainly fits all the circumstances of the play, and in my case makes the motivations and behaviour patterns of the characters easier to interpret.

POZZO	Waiting? So you were waiting for him?
VLADIMIR	Well you see—
POZZO	Here? On my land?
VLADIMIR	We didn't intend any harm.
ESTRAGON	We meant well.
POZZO	The road is free to all.
VLADIMIR	That's how we looked at it.
POZZO	It's a disgrace. But there you are.
ESTRAGON	Nothing we can do about it.
POZZO	(*with magnanimous gesture*) Let's say no more about it.

This passage for me completely sums up Pozzo's relationship with the two tramps.

The character of Lucky, on the other hand, I see in much the same terms as it was interpreted in France; a creature of ultimate degradation and suffering. The script is fairly specific about certain things. First of all Lucky must be in a state of physical debilitation so extreme that when Pozzo stops short on his first entrance, and tautens the rope, Lucky falls with all his baggage. Secondly, he must have long white hair.

POZZO That was nearly sixty years ago. . . . (*He consults his watch*) Yes, nearly sixty. (*Drawing himself up proudly.*) You wouldn't think it to look at me, would you? Compared to him I look like a young man. No? (*Pause*) Hat! (*Lucky puts down the basket and takes off his hat. His long white hair falls about his face.*)

The only aspect of Lucky not covered in the stage directions is his clothes. In this I followed Roger Blin's lead, by giving him a sort of old-fashioned footman's coat and knee breeches. There are in Ireland a number of Anglo-Irish aristocratic families, who live in grand, but excessively delapidated mansions, and it is not unusual for them to follow all the mores of their well-to-do English counterparts, without nearly enough money to do the thing properly. For this reason, I thought it would fit in with my conception of the Pozzo-Lucky relationship to have Lucky's elaborate livery moth-eaten and tattered.

Curiously enough, it was Lucky's conception and performance which seemed to make the most impact in my English production of the play. This was possibly due to the fact that in the original London production the part was played much younger in a sort of Boots costume with green baize apron, and not nearly so debilitated. A lot of very horrifying and emotionally harsh plays have been presented in London since 1955, and these have toughened West End audiences. From something that Donald Albery said to me during the run of the original *Godot*, I suspect that parts of the play were specially softened for English consumption at that time, and it is more than likely that if this is the case the conception of Lucky was part of a deliberate scheme. The particularly brutal moments of the play, where Lucky is viciously kicked, in Act One by Pozzo, and in Act Two by Estragon, are of course made much more horrifying if Lucky has the general aspect of an inmate of Belsen. It may be true that in 1955 this would simply have had the effect of driving the well-fed patrons out of the theatre.

Lucky's speech, too, seemed to make a very great impression on English audiences. Of course, having produced five previous Luckys, I was in a position to give Derek Young more detailed guidance than if I had been coming at the play for the first time. But he certainly responded magnificently to my suggestions, worked very hard and gave a really memorable performance. I use the words 'work hard' advisedly, because to play Lucky certainly makes very unusual demands on an actor. He is pulled about by the rope, thrown heavily on the stage, and kicked. With the best will in the world and the most expert faking, it is not always possible to avoid hurting him.

In attacking the long speech within the framework of Beckett's instructions, which are not particularly explicit at this point, I made the following suggestions. For the phrases with some sort of emotional connotation, I said that he should play them in a way that suggested the emotion implied in the words. For instance, 'loves us dearly' was to be played sentimentally and softly; 'plunged in torment, plunged in fire whose fire flames' in a manner suggesting extreme suffering; 'heaven so blue still and calm so calm with a calm' drawn out, smoothly and gently; 'the great cold the great dark' shiveringly, and so forth. In the linking passages, such as 'which even though intermittent is better than nothing', he should speak quickly, in a dry manner suggestive of a caricatured University professor lecturing. I got him to vary the tempo in this way until the line 'in the year of their Lord six hundred and something', after which he was to shout the lines as vigorously and rapidly as possible. The reactions of the tramps and Pozzo were to be as specifically outlined by Beckett, with the addition that the tramps should react shocked to 'Fartov and Belcher', and 'Feckham'. I made the phrase, 'the skull the skull the skull the skull' the signal for the all-out attack by the others in their efforts to stop the now frenzied spate of words.

In Raymond Williams's review of this production in the *New Statesman*, he said:

'Cut across by compulsion and fatigue as well as by the babble of scraps from the schoolmen and scientific scholarship, this speech is still central. It is worth ignoring these scraps and following the main line:

Given the existence of a personal God . . . who . . . loves us dearly with some exceptions, for reasons unknown but time will tell and suffers . . . with those who . . . are plunged in torment . . . and considering . . . that . . . it is established beyond all doubt . . . that man . . . in spite of the progress . . . wastes and pines . . . and considering what is more much more grave . . . the great cold the great dark the air and the earth abode of stones in the great world . . . alas alas on on . . . to shrink pine waste . . . alas alas on on the skull the skull the skull . . .

This traditional vision of man's decline into death is confused and unfinished, on the edge of breakdown but not broken down altogether, and the play was greatly strengthened by its clear speaking (the easy alternative is gabble and horseplay).'

I think the foregoing is quite a clever analysis of the speech, but in this and in the rest of the play the actors and myself never worried about the academic or philosophical implications of the lines, but always followed our emotional instincts. Over these, with both casts, we never seemed to have any doubts or disagreements. The play has so many intellectual implications, either intentional or accidental, that if actors and producers were to try and approach their work on any sort of an academic basis, it would lead to confusion and stilting of the easy flow of the dialogue, which in my view is essential to any dramatic performance. 'Leave all that to the newspapermen' I used to say, 'they get paid for it, you get paid for acting.'

Of all the plays that I have ever produced, it is the most difficult for the smooth and natural accomplishment of the author's very explicit instructions regarding stage business. I was very fortunate in having Nigel Fitzgerald for my second production of the play, because the timing of his manœuvres with pipe, matches, vaporizer, basket, whip, rope and watch, are highly intricate and take weeks of rehearsal if they are to be accomplished as naturally as the stage direction demands. What we used to call 'the heap', too, in Act Two, where Lucky collapses with Pozzo on top of him, and Vladimir and Estragon subsequently follow suit, makes enormous demands on the physical precision and stamina of the actors, and requires endless practice and experiment if it is to be carried out in any way convincingly.

In approaching the décor for *Godot* there are considerable pointers in the script. As mentioned before, the initial directions say:

'A country road. A tree. Evening'.

but there are references in the text which can help the designer.

ESTRAGON   Charming spot. (*He turns, advancing to front, halts facing auditorium.*) Inspiring prospects.

VLADIMIR   He said by the tree. (*They look at the tree.*) Do you see any others?

ESTRAGON   What is it?

VLADIMIR   I don't know. A willow.

ESTRAGON   Where are the leaves?

VLADIMIR   It must be dead.

ESTRAGON   No more weeping.

VLADIMIR   Or perhaps it's not the season.

ESTRAGON   Looks to me more like a bush.

VLADIMIR   A shrub.

ESTRAGON   A bush.

VLADIMIR   What are you insinuating. That we've come to the wrong place?

and

VLADIMIR   (*looking round*) You recognize the place?

ESTRAGON   I didn't say that.

VLADIMIR   Well?

ESTRAGON   That makes no difference.

VLADIMIR   All the same . . . that tree . . . (*turning towards auditorium*) that bog . . .

VLADIMIR   Where else do you think? Do you not recognize the place?

ESTRAGON   (*suddenly furious*) Recognize! What is there to
        recognize?

and

POZZO   What is it like?
VLADIMIR   (*looking round*) It's indescribable. It's like noth-
        ing. There's nothing. There's a tree.

From the foregoing quotations from the dialogue,
it would seem to be obvious that the tree is the only
recognizable feature. It is also important that the
tree should be small enough to make it completely
impractical as a gallows. I think the whole point of
the two hanging sequences (one in each act) is that
there shouldn't be any feasibility whatsoever in the
project. At the same time, any designer will insist
that, because it is the focal point, the tree should be
big enough in relation to the total size of the stage to
take the eye.

I didn't see Roger Blin's Paris production at the
beginning of the run, but when I did see it the décor
consisted simply of some pieces of light green cloth
(suspiciously like old double sheets) hung around the
back and sides of the stage. This gave an exceptionally
dreary effect, but in my view it looked amateurish.
Some years ago, I had an argument with Sam on this
point. He emphatically approved of this arrangement,
while I maintained that it should be possible to give
the effect of negative dreariness on the stage without
actually appearing not to have bothered, as was the
case in the Babylone. We agreed to differ, and in my
Pike production I designed the setting myself, which
consisted of a back cloth and wings painted with
daubs of green, black and brown paint, very vaguely

suggestive of Irish bogland and gloomy sky. In the Criterion, the designer made the set much more elaborate, with various debris suggestive of a rubbish dump, and with an extremely interesting, but in my view too large and practical a stage tree. At the back, he used a cyclorama, as far as I can remember. At any rate, the total effect was far too elaborate and interesting.

When I came to discuss the décor for the Theatre Workshop production with John Ryan, he produced for me an extremely interesting design, involving again the use of the cyclorama, barbed wire and a rather decorative roadside bank running right across the stage. This I vetoed point-blank, so he very graciously produced another design, using a back-cloth painted in browns and very dark greys, with a vague impression of roughly horizontal lines and a few little white dots. We found a small real tree, as in Dublin, and the bank or mound on which Estragon sits was small and angular. The total effect was quite abstract, with a suggestion of peat and limestone, together with a hint of Outer Space. Words cannot in any way convey the impression of an abstract work of art, but the ultimate result was completely negative and dreary, while at the same time professional and neat. I regarded it as a tribute to John's achievement that not one of the newspaper reviews so much as mentioned the décor, even though this may have been somewhat galling for him. As the theatre is a co-operative art, ultimately depending from the public's viewpoint upon the author's lines spoken by the actors, I think that all décor, lighting and production should be subservient to this end. From time to time

in recent theatrical history, various producers, de-
signers and stage-lighting enthusiasts have adopted
more dominant roles than I believe are right for real
artistic achievement.

The lighting in *Waiting for Godot* plays rather an
important role in assisting the mood at the end of
each act. Each act can be divided into well-defined
sections. First, the two tramps endeavouring to pass
the time. Secondly, the Pozzo and Lucky diversion.
Thirdly, the arrival and departure of the Boy; and
fourthly, the falling of night and the decision to wait
on till the next day. In Act One, the first section is
fairly short—merely long enough to get the audience
into the mood of the tramps in their vigil, but not so
long as to become boring. In this section in Act Two,
Beckett has used, unconsciously perhaps, the radio
comedy show technique of the family joke. The
audience is now aware of the situation, and is amused
simply by the spectacle of the continued frantic en-
deavours of the tramps to pass the time. There are
also, as in a radio show, gags based on references to
Pozzo and Lucky, such as:

VLADIMIR Will you not play?
ESTRAGON Play at what?
VLADIMIR We could play at Pozzo and Lucky.

In Section Three, the arrival of the Boy with his
unsatisfactory message puts an immediate end to all
suggestion of comedy, and the final section in each
case should be deeply moving and round off the act
in a minor key *decrescendo*. Some audiences can become very giggly during the play, and the abrupt
change of lighting assists producer and actors to con-

133

trol this tendency, and to impose on them the right mood. Here, it is permissible—even desirable that the tree and tramps be dimly and impressively lit, in contrast to the negative dreariness of the preceding sections and the concluding

VLADIMIR   Well? Shall we go?
ESTRAGON   Yes. Let's go.

should be spoken in a tableau of absolute stillness and haunting beauty.

One aspect of the presentation about which the author has very strong views are the pauses. This immediately raises production problems for the English-speaking director. The English, Irish and, I imagine, American audiences have got into the habit of expecting a fast-moving production with the dialogue at all times rattling along at a spanking pace, only halted by very definite and well-defined movement or business. Throughout *Waiting for Godot* the reader will frequently come across the instruction:

Silence.

Sam Beckett means this direction to be taken literally, and if his wishes are to be followed it is necessary for the dialogue immediately before and after such an instruction to be particularly brisk. Peter Hall, in his original London production, took what I believe was an unsatisfactory, easy way out. He filled the more important pauses with a sort of heavenly music. In my opinion, this takes away from the stark quality of the play. I gather from talking recently to Peter that he has now come round to this view himself.

Actually, it was producing *Waiting for Godot* on

these terms that got me thinking about the nature of dramatic dialogue. The human mind moves much quicker than the vocal chords, and in average conversation people cut in on one another's sentences much more than you would imagine. Thus in the exchange:

JOHN   Let's go to *Waiting for Godot* tonight.
MARY   But we promised to go and see the Murphys.

Mary realizes that John is going to say, 'Waiting for Godot' by the time he has spoken the word 'waiting' (perhaps because they were both reading the review of the play that morning) and if the dialogue is to sound realistic, she will have formulated her sentence and commenced speaking at the latest by the time he had spoken the 'to' of 'tonight'. However, when she makes her statement, this floors John, and it may take him a couple of seconds before he replies.

Since becoming aware of this, I have tried to have the dialogue in all my productions spoken in sporadic fits and starts, with occasional pauses to allow the characters and the audience to adjust their thoughts. That I sometimes, at any rate, succeed, is borne out by the following remarks of Ronald Mavor, writing in the *Scotsman* about my production of Diego Fabbri's *Inquisition* in the Dublin Theatre Festival of 1959: '. . . And indeed there were many times during the play when—perhaps due to the director's fondness for sudden pauses and sudden explosions of words— I had the strange impression that I was watching a play in French.'

One could ramble on for many more pages about the artistic and technical problems of producing these plays, and like Pozzo:

'I don't seem to be able . . . (*long hesitation*) . . . to depart.'

However, I will save up any other comments I have for my concluding chapter. Having so far dealt with the general theatrical situation at the time the plays were first presented, with some biographical details of the authors, and with my own approach to putting their work on the stage, I now intend to try and give the reader a personal view of an incident which is symptomatic of the Dublin theatrical scene.

I include the story of this incident in this book, partly because it is a good story and this is the first opportunity I have had to tell it properly, but mainly because it serves to illustrate an attitude of mind of a section of the Irish population which in an indirect way produces rebels against it such as Brendan Behan and Sam Beckett.

Brendan undoubtedly is at the spearhead of a revival of the bawdry of Restoration comedy, and his more recent writing is quite as outrageous and perhaps even more exuberant than the cuckoldry farces of that period. Sam Beckett, in his own more schoolmasterly way, is just as insistent on the inclusion in his plays and novels of what is, to average *bourgeois* standards, blasphemy and lavatory humour.

The ancient Gaelic race, if one is to judge from such writing as *The Midnight Court* and other works of a like nature, took an immense delight in sex and bawdry in general. This aspect of Gaelic writing has been carefully screened from the modern 'Gaelicly Revived' Irish youth.

The change in the outlook of the average Irishman was brought about by the fusion of English 'middle-class morality' with oppressed Catholicism. It first manifested itself at the end of the last century with the fall os Parnell (in the political field) and with the *Playboy of the Western World* riots in the Abbey Theatre in the early 1900's. Nowadays, the Irish writing which attracts critical attention abroad is almost inevitably banned by our ubiquitous Censorship of Publications Board. Consequently there exists what almost amounts to a neurosis among our men of letters. The attitude of, say, Frank O'Connor to Ireland in general and Cork in particular is a good case in point.

The theatre, because of its vividness as an art form seems to be particularly susceptible to the attention of that powerful body of opinion, Ireland's 'lay clerics'. That the story related in the following chapter has no direct bearing on Samuel Beckett or Brendan Behan is merely coincidental.

CHAPTER V

'THE ROSE TATTOO'

∿∿

WHEN, in the early thirties, Eamonn de Valera's Republican Party (Fianna Fáil) decided to enter constitutional politics, he started a national newspaper, the *Irish Press*. This was in order to give the party a public mouthpiece and to counteract the effect of the *Irish Independent*, which although vigorous in its condemnation of the 1916 Rising, since the Treaty had been firm in its support of Cosgrave's Free State Government. So it was with not a little self-satisfaction that, on the 13th May 1957, I read the concluding lines of the *Irish Press* review of *The Rose Tattoo*, which was the opening play of the first Dublin Theatre Festival. 'Once again, the Pike must be highly recommended for giving Dublin a remarkable piece of theatre.'

By this time, the theatre had been in existence for nearly four years. We had had our successes with Brendan Behan and Sam Beckett. We had had favourable comment on the feature pages of foreign newspapers and periodicals; and now it looked as if we were to become the show-piece of the Theatre Festival, officially sponsored by Bord Failte, the State Tourist Board. Apart from various advances in the political field, the Government had, over the past few years, initiated, through Bord Failte, several projects calculated to enhance Ireland's reputation as a cultural centre. Of these projects, the Theatre Festival seemed most likely to succeed. Ireland already had a sound international reputation in the theatrical field; the names of the Abbey and the Gate were world famous; and apart from horses, the word 'theatre' would probably be the first thing to spring to the mind of an educated foreigner, if asked what he knew of our country.

During the opening week of the Festival, therefore, the signs were all very good. Our own production was highly praised in all the Irish newspapers, and the Public Relations Department of the Tourist Board were constantly on the telephone to my wife, begging for seats for this or that distinguished foreign journalist. The other theatres also received high praise, particularly Hilton Edwards's production of a revival of Denis Johnston's expressionist *The Old Lady Says No*. For the first time in my life, I was learning of the pleasures of official V.I.P. treatment. As theatre owners, myself and my wife were invited everywhere, and when we weren't drinking cocktails with the diplomatic corps, we were being shaken warmly by the hand by Government ministers and Tourist Board officials. On the Sunday following our opening, a glowing notice from Harold Hobson in Britain's leading, cultural Sunday paper seemed to imply that little Herbert Lane was on the way to becoming as distinguished a thoroughfare as Abbey Street or Cavendish Row.

Despite our official Festival guarantee—subsidy—

the capacity of the Pike, combined with the large numbers in the cast, meant that my share of the profits only amounted to about seven pounds weekly. So I approached the late Lord Longford for permission to transfer *The Rose Tattoo* into the Gate Theatre after the conclusion of the official two weeks of the Festival. To this he agreed, and on the second Tuesday after we had opened, I was upstairs in the men's dressing-room of the Pike, discussing the financial arrangements for the Gate Theatre with a member of the cast. Having reached a delicate stage in my negotiations, I was inclined to be a little impatient when told that I was wanted downstairs. My impatience was not decreased when my wife, never the most tranquil of people, announced with some agitation that it was an inspector of police who wanted to see me. The narrowness of Herbert Lane, combined with the large number of garage doors which are frequently blocked by the cars of our patrons, meant that the appearance of a policeman, accompanied by an irate neighbour, was a fairly common occurrence.

However, she ultimately prevailed upon me to abandon my difference-splitting and present myself to a large, stern-looking Inspector Ward. Ponderously, the inspector read to me from a typewritten sheet, which—stripped of its official sounding phrases—boiled down to a demand that we should immediately cancel that night's performance, due to commence in about fifteen minutes. If not, both my wife and I would be arrested. It had been 'brought to their attention' that the play contained 'objectionable passages'. By whom, and which passages, we were unable to discover. Indeed to this day, we have been unable to discover, although we have heard many rumours and theories on the subject.

The inspector interrupted the horrified silence to which I was reduced by, 'Do you intend continuing the presentation of this play?' He somehow managed to say 'play' as if it were a dirty word. From that moment, I was plunged into a nightmare of melo-drama which was to continue for over a year. The plays I had produced in the Pike had not been of the Agatha Christie variety, so I had to rely on my youth-ful memories of Edward G. Robinson and Spencer Tracy for guidance in such a situation. 'I couldn't answer that without consulting my solicitor,' was the best I could manage. While the good inspector digested this, I told my wife to have them take up the curtain. It went up ten minutes late that night.

Some time previously, I had had occasion to take legal advice concerning the rights of *The Quare Fellow*, and when I was unable to get through to my own solicitor on the telephone, Con Lehane, who had represented Brendan with considerable agility on that occasion immediately came to my mind. Con, since his earliest youth had been associated with Republi-canism, and was a close colleague of Sean MacBride. His experience in dealing with the highly explosive legal side of their quasi-military activities made him an admirable chief of staff for this particular battle. 'Ask the inspector to wait,' he said, 'I will be down in about twenty minutes.'

During rehearsal, Brendan Smith, the Festival director, had 'phoned me one day in some agitation to say that he had received a letter from a body called the 'League of Decency' (which none of us had ever

heard of) complaining that *The Rose Tattoo* 'advo-
cated the use of birth control by unnatural means'.
This was so silly that I was inclined to regard the
whole thing as a joke. To satisfy him, however, I put
him in touch with Pat Nolan, the actor playing the
male lead, who is a very devout Catholic, and had to
my certain knowledge turned down various parts in
the past on grounds of their religious or moral shortcomings. After Pat had talked to Mr. Smith, the latter
caused the League's letter to be 'marked as read' in the
minutes of his committee. None of us had given the
matter another thought.

My own view of the play is that it is in fact very
deeply and subtly complimentary to Roman Catholicism, and Gabriel Fallon, one-time critic of the Irish
Catholic weekly, *The Standard*, and now a director of
the Abbey Theatre, wrote in the *Evening Press*, '*The
Rose Tattoo* gives rise to the possibility that the Irish
(deep down at all events) have much in common with
the Sicilians. Or is it that Mr. Williams has unexpec-
tedly touched universality in this play? Go and see it.
It will be well worth your while.'

It was obvious to me, although this was never said by
any of the prosecution lawyers, or by the police, that
the spark which ignited the whole affair was the scene
in which the widow Serafina rejects the advances
of her lorry driver suitor, whom she, by implica-
tion, is going to marry at the end of the play. In this
scene, the lorry driver seems to be making some progress towards a pre-marital seduction. When a small
packet falls from his pocket, Serafina's deep, almost
instinctive religious conviction is so strong that, even
though her passions are aroused, her disgust at the

suggestion that he is proposing to make use of something basically repugnant to Catholic dogma, over-
comes her fiery Southern nature. She devotes the
rest of the scene to enraged vituperation, and sends
the uncouth and bewildered Alvaro about his business.
There are reasons to believe that none of the persons
responsible for the initiation of the police action were
in possession of any copy of the script, and that all
those dealing with the affair were working simply on
second- or third-hand information, provided by
people prejudiced against the Theatre in general, and
Tennessee Williams in particular.

In my production, I contrived this scene—as I
thought—in such a way that any persons not sophisticated enough to appreciate the implications of the
situation would remain in ignorance as to what was
supposed to have taken place. Those Catholics who
understood would, I felt, appreciate the implied
compliment to the Faith. That I was largely successful in my attempt to handle these more delicate matters without offence is borne out by Mr. Hobson's
description of the direction as being of 'outstanding
discrimination'. In the subsequent proceedings, it
came to light that plain-clothes detectives had attended the second night performance of the play,
having been unable to get seats for the opening. That
they did not have the remotest appreciation of these
finer points was patently obvious from their demeanour in court.

When Con arrived, he asked the inspector to show
him the document from which he had been reading.
The inspector refused to do this, but under pressure,
agreed to read it aloud again. Con took it down and

subsequently wrote a letter to the Deputy Commissioner of Police (from whom the document had apparently emanated) asking to have the 'offensive passages' named. At this point I felt that, in order to save the Festival and the country at large from ridicule in the eyes of the world, I would be prepared to make some cuts; although naturally I felt that this would spoil the delicate artistic balance of the play. The inspector, however, insisted that the play must come off before any such discussions took place. I realized from his manner that if the play did come off, the ponderous, bureaucratic delays, would almost certainly spin out over the remaining few days of the Festival, and the newspapers would inevitably over-dramatize the affair. At any time, in fact, during the previous week, had some responsible official of the Department of Justice, or even the Government, approached me with a view to modifying the production in any way, I would have agreed—albeit reluctantly—rather than bring the entire Festival unfavourable publicity.

Convinced that someone was acting without the knowledge of his superiors, we still felt that the thing might be hard to stop once started, though even then, we imagined that the Department of Justice would thank us for saving them from making fools of themselves. We decided not to waste time with intermediaries. As chairman of the Dublin Tostal Council, Robert Briscoe, then Lord Mayor, was our patron and guarantor. Obviously he could have all this nonsense squashed. When we finally contacted him by telephone on the Wednesday morning, we got a further shock. He was not only unsympathetic and unwilling to help. He attacked me for 'daring to present such a play'—which I may say, he had not seen.

The next two days passed in a haze of unreality. Determined not to alarm the cast, I kept our worries from them, while frantically contacting everyone who might help at the highest levels. Honesty, however, compelled me to acquaint Lord Longford of the situation. He maintained that the presentation of the play would prejudice his own legal battles over the re-licensing of the Gate, and said that he could not fulfil his contract with us to present the play the following week. By putting cancellation notices in the Press, he forced me to release the whole story by way of explanation, a step I had hoped to avoid lest it tie the hands of potential rescuers in official or semi-official circles.

Thursday was my eldest daughter's birthday, and I took a half day's leave from the army and brought herself, her sisters, and some friends to the zoo. Appropriately enough, it was in the monkey house that we drafted a manifesto for the newspapers. I then sent my wife and the children home, and went down to Con Lehane's office to get his approval for the manifesto, which merely stated the facts as they had occurred and maintained my view that the play was in no way objectionable. While I was there, he received by special messenger from Dublin Castle the Deputy Commissioner's reply to the letter he had sent two days previously. This reply merely said that in view of my refusal to take off the play, the matter was 'being dealt with by the proper authorities according to law'.

My instinct of the last couple of days that the whole affair would be of fantastic interest to the Press, was correct. Even as I discussed the Deputy Commissioner's reply with Con, the intercom. on his desk buzzed. 'A Mr. Brady is downstairs to see you,' said the voice of his secretary. Lord Beaverbrook's Dublin representative was already on the job.

When my statement had been typed, I shot out of the office, pausing only to hand Mr. Brady a copy of my statement. Con had said that from the tone of the Deputy Commissioner's letter, we might expect some action that night, and I wanted to get my statement around the newspapers before 'the due processes of law' rendered me incommunicado. In most of the reporters' rooms of the Dublin newspapers I was a fairly familiar figure, as I frequently helped out my P.R.O. in the dissemination of theatre publicity; and several of them just took the paper casually, expecting to find the usual theatrical hand-out for the gossip columnists. Unfortunately, I didn't have the time or the inclination to wait and watch their eyes popping, as they read the startling facts.

When I arrived home my wife had already left for the theatre and I sat down gloomily to eat the baked beans she had left for me in the oven. Suddenly the 'phone rang. It was Aiden McGuire, the house manager of the Pike. 'They've come!' he said, in great agitation. 'Who?' I asked. 'The police. They're in squad cars at either end of the lane, waiting for you. Carol suggests that you come down through Nicholsons! Then they won't be able to get you until you reach the theatre.' The Pike box-office is in a mews building opposite the theatre and can be reached from

13. A scene from *The Rose Tattoo*.

14(a). '. . . slamming the door on Aiden's wrist'.

14(b). '. . . I must accompany him to Bridewell'.

the Nicholson's house in Herbert Place. Luckily, we were on very friendly terms with the family.

I had tried to avoid publicity as long as possible, but now that the die was cast, I was determined that the publicity should be exploited to our advantage. With what appeared to be the entire forces of the State arrayed against me, my only hope of avoiding disgrace and imprisonment seemed to be to get the public on my side. When I arrived at the theatre, having successfully dodged the posse, there was a battery of some eight camera-men lined up across the lane.

For a while, nothing happened, but then somehow the news that I had arrived penetrated to the Law. A burly detective, traditionally dressed in raincoat and trilby hat, came awkwardly down the lane. He approached me. 'Detective Inspector Scanlon would like to see you at the end of the lane,' he said. By this time the news cameras were clicking and the unhappy detective put his arm across his face in a vain attempt to protect his anonymity. 'You can tell Inspector Scanlon', I replied, 'that if he wants me, I am here.' There was a further delay while the detective retired to consult with his superiors. Meanwhile, inside the theatre, a packed house attentively watched the Tennessee Williams's piece, ignorant of the real life drama that was taking place outside.

Then a large, black squad car, containing four very well built and formidable plain-clothes men came slowly down the lane. Again, the newsmen raised their cameras. The police got out of the car and converged on me. I am five foot eleven and a half, and pretty solid, but beside these hefty limbs of the law I felt like a fourteen-year-old undernourished Teddy

Boy. They demanded that I accompany them into the box-office, out of the hearing of Aiden McGuire and my wife, and when I demurred, two of the biggest dragged me in forcibly, pushing my wife violently back into the lane and slamming the door on Aiden's wrist, which was swollen for some days afterwards. This exhibition was slickly photographed by the Press.

Inspector Scanlon announced that he was arresting me on a warrant sworn that afternoon, which he showed me. He then said that I must accompany him to the Bridewell, the remand prison attached to the Dublin District Court. During the few minutes before they had arrived I had arranged that Con be informed. He had instructed that someone be found as bailsman. One of the people we had contacted with a view to getting the matter cleared up before it had reached the ears of the public, was a former Fianna Fáil Senator, Michael ffrench O'Carroll, who is a distinguished Dublin doctor and had been a classmate of mine at University. He had readily agreed to go bail, should the need arise.

On arrival at the Bridewell I was formally charged with 'presenting for gain an indecent and profane performance'. This was the first intimation that I had received of the exact nature of my alleged crime. Then I was made turn out my pockets, and all sharp instruments, such as my nail clippers, keys and cigarette lighter were removed from me and I was taken to a cell. After some time a warder brought me out again and told me that my solicitor had come to see me. Con's face was gloomy.

'They're giving you the full works,' he said.

'They've arrested you on a summary warrant.' He
told me that this warrant, normally reserved for
dangerous I.R.A. men and armed criminals, pro-
cluded the granting of bail until such time as I had
appeared in court. He said that I was entitled to get a
meal sent in at my own expense, and slipped me some
cigarettes and matches. 'I'll see you in the morning,
before you're brought to court.' I asked him if I
could see Carol to make arrangements to get a substitute for me in the *Late Night Revue*. (This was still
running each night, half an hour after the conclusion
of *The Rose Tattoo*, and I was appearing in a couple of
numbers.) He replied that I could see nobody except
him, and that he would deliver my suggestions to
Carol and give her what help he could to see that
they were carried out. I heard afterwards that she
made the necessary arrangements with considerable
efficiency, and had gone on stage before the curtain
went up to announce, 'Ladies and Gentlemen, owing
to the unavoidable arrest of Mr. Alan Simpson, his
parts in tonight's performance will be played by Mr.
Charles Roberts.' When the laugh had died down,
she told them the circumstances of the arrest, quoting
from our manifesto, and was loudly cheered.

A rather surly warder obtained a meal for me,
which I consumed without relish. Later, he was replaced by a more genial character, who inquired
with sincere sympathy if it were naked women I was
in for. When I told him it wasn't, he sadly remarked
that 'they' were 'very funny in this country about
them things'. He then gave practical vent to his sympathy by obtaining me a miniature bottle of Irish
whiskey, 'a Baby Power'.

I spent a miserable night in the cell. The fast moving melodrama of the period in between Inspector Ward's visit to the theatre and my arrest, had not given me much time for reflection. Con had told me that the maximum penalty for someone convicted of my alleged crime was two years' imprisonment. Even if I only received a nominal sentence, conviction of an indictable offence would mean automatic dismissal from the Army and loss of pension rights. The nineteenth-century sex neurosis of the Irish people would immediately bracket me in the category of sex criminals. To be caught embezzling, or drunk in charge of a vehicle, is a matter for sympathy or even laughter; and to be imprisoned for political offences is regarded as an honourable apprenticeship to public life. But a man or woman convicted of anything even remotely involving sex is treated as a social pariah and an outcast, and his crime can only be discussed by dark hints in lowered voices.

The contrast between my present predicament and the outlook only a few days previously was enormous. Then, I had been, from nine to five, an army officer, accustomed to respect and even deference, in and outside the Army, and after five, a newly elected member of the theatrical *élite*. I didn't sleep at all that night, and it wasn't because of the hardness of the bed. By the morning, my morale was very low.

Breakfast, supplied by the State, consisting of a piece of bread and a mug of dubious tea, did little to cheer me. Shortly before eleven o'clock I was led by an underground passage to a dimly lit, subterranean, iron-barred ante-room directly beneath the court. Here, I was placed in the charge of a very pleasant detective. As fellow-servants of the State we had quite an interesting discussion on comparative conditions between the Police and the Army, and the 'Three Ps'. ('The Three Ps' are what Brendan says, in *The Quare Fellow*, should be the only proper topic of conversation for Civil Servants. . . . Pay, Pension and Promotion.) I elicited from him the information that he had in fact attended *The Rose Tattoo*, but when I tried to obtain his real views on the subject he shut up like a clam.

Shortly before I was due to go up to court, Con appeared. He was even gloomier and sterner than he had been the night before. James Heavey, a mutual barrister friend of ours, whom he had briefed to appear for me, had been speaking to the Chief State Solicitor. He had been informed that if, at this juncture, I were to give an undertaking in court that there would be no further performances of the play, the whole matter would be dropped. Were I to refuse, not merely would the State proceed with the indictment, but also they would oppose bail. This, Con said, could mean imprisonment for anything up to six weeks before the case could be heard.

'What do you advise?' I asked him. 'As your solicitor, I must advise you to give the undertaking.' 'But as a friend?' I asked. I thought I detected a flicker of a smile in his eyes. 'I am here as your solicitor,' he said impassively. I thought for a moment. Even after the brainwashing effect of my night in the cell, I was still convinced that the play was worthy of the Festival and in no way offensive. If I gave up now, and took the play off, it would be like an admission of guilt, and no one would ever believe that the show was anything but grossly indecent. 'Tell them I will give no such undertaking,' I said. Con smiled slightly, 'I thought you might say that, but I didn't want to influence you.'

After a further wait, my detective escort brought me up the staircase which ejects defendants suddenly into the middle of the light and airy courtroom, like so many bewildered moles. I was led into the dock, where I was to spend so many happy hours over the next twelve months. When my eyes became accustomed to the light, I gradually noticed that the court seemed to be filled with friendly faces. Apart from my wife and Aiden McGuire, there was nearly the whole cast of the play and a number of other friends and sympathizers.

The proceedings were fairly lengthy, as there were two adjournments for the prosecution to consult with the Attorney-General's Office. I was fortunate in the person of the District Justice before whom I was appearing. Although unknown to me, he turned out to be a cultured man and a distinguished amateur Shakespearian actor. Had he not regarded my position with sympathy, I should almost certainly have found myself back in my cell, for the State solicitor was most vigorous in his efforts to have bail refused. Words like 'lewd', 'indecent', 'offensive', 'corruption', 'morality', spat from his mouth like machine-gun bullets. But the District Justice was firm. He said after one of the adjournments, that he had made inquiries, and a colleague was available to hear the case that day. But the State solicitor said that his witnesses were scattered over the city and could not be assembled quickly. In the course of his argument he also made thinly veiled threats against the liberty of the cast. 'If bail was granted,' he said, 'the defendant, as producer and director of the play, would, it was reasonable to believe, continue with the play. That would be another offence with which he could again be charged, as indeed could everybody associated with it.' After considerable further argument, the date for the hearing was fixed for July 4th. Bail was fixed at £100, fifty from myself and fifty from an independent surety. A friend volunteered to be the independant surety. He was Commandant Seamus Heron, the Eastern Command Legal Officer, and grandson of James Connolly.

I had been subjected to so many rapid changes of climate that emotionally I was unable to appreciate the warm welcome that awaited me outside the court. I received treatment normally accorded to the captain of the winning side of an international football match. A battery of news cameras, newsreel cameras, and television cameras photographed me being shaken by the hand, kissed by my wife, and surrounded by the cast, and I was practically chaired to the gate. However, any relief this may have offered to my battered nerves was short lived. Walking down O'Connell Street soon afterwards, we purchased the early editions of the evening papers. 'Alleged indecent and profane performance'—'Producer in Court'—'Indecent and profane performance charge'—'Attorney-General alleges play was lewd, indecent, and offensive'. These, in inch-high heavy type, were some of the phrases that stared out at me from the page. Each story was accompanied by large and easily recognizable photographs. I felt people looking curiously at me. When I caught their eye, they would hastily look away. It is the business of everyone in the theatre to court publicity on every possible occasion for professional reasons, but this was different. I had achieved notoriety overnight.

The first job to be done was to call the cast together and find out if they were prepared to risk arrest and continue the play. I was unhappy about this. With such a large cast, it had been necessary to employ a few people with jobs outside the theatre. One or two of them were Civil Servants. They were in the same position as myself, namely, that if they were charged and convicted, they could well find themselves facing automatic dismissal. I decided that the only thing to do was to hold a meeting and get their views.

In the meantime, however, Kate Binchy, who was playing the part of Serafina's teenage daughter, called on me in some distress. Her father was a judge and felt that if he allowed his daughter, a minor, to take part in what would in fact be an open defiance of the Courts, it would place him in an impossible position. Kate was prepared to disobey her father, and even to go and stay with friends. I felt I could not accept her offer, much as I was tempted to do so, and my thirty-four-year-old wife rather unhappily volunteered to play the fifteen-year-old girl, should we go on with the show. Subsequently, when I invited Kate to play in Belfast, which is out of the jurisdiction of the Irish Courts, her father agreed that she should do so, even though the case was still *sub judice* and the newspapers were bound to comment on his change of heart. To satisfy his conscience he got her to consult a Jesuit friend. The priest pronounced *The Rose Tattoo* an excellent play.

At six o'clock we held the cast meeting. Except for one actor, who held an unestablished, non-pension-able post as a Cultural Adviser to a State body, and who was liable to dismissal at a week's notice, every-one was determined to carry on. This actor bravely agreed to abide by the majority decision, even though he was very worried about the possible reaction of his superiors. The electrician was a sergeant in my own Army unit. He was most enthusiastic to remain at his post, but I told him that if there were any signs of the police taking names or making arrests, he was to hide on the fly rail and, if necessary, escape through a back window before he could be identified.

Con had told me that from a legal point of view it would be advisable for me not to be near the theatre during the performance, so I booked a seat for *The Old Lady Says No* and thereby missed the strange hap-penings at Herbert Lane that night. I enjoyed the first act of Hilton's dynamic production, but in the inter-val some hysterical rumourmonger met me in Groome's Hotel. 'They have arrested the entire cast of the play and taken them off to the Bridewell in two black Marias,' she told me. I frantically tried to 'phone the theatre, but the line of course was out of order. I remained drinking with Joe Groome, the Secretary of the Fianna Fáil Party, and his wife, until the time that the show should be down in Herbert Lane.

When I arrived I was greeted at the end of the lane by a car-load of Army officers, some of them in uniform, who had come there for the purpose of defending me against any further attacks by the police. Down at the Pike all was comparatively quiet. The cast had not been arrested and the performance had taken place. Before the performance, Inspector Scanlon had seen each actor personally and renewed the threats of prosecution. In the Pike auditorium, a number of very obvious plain-clothes detectives lined the walls. In the lane a large crowd had assembled to demonstrate on our behalf. Among them were many notabilities, including a well-known District Justice and Brendan Behan. The latter regaled the assembly with patriotic and revolutionary airs. The goat which appears in the play was kept in an adjoining garage till the last possible moment, on account of its fondness for devouring the costumes of female members of the cast awaiting their cues. When it was led into the theatre Brendan's ready wit immediately saw it as a further 'Cue for Song' and burst into a spirited rendition of 'The Peeler and the Goat'.

The cast was inclined to be hysterical and frequently had to shout to make themselves heard above the din created by our supporters outside. In his dressing-room, the ten-year-old boy who played Bruno kept crying that he didn't want to go to jail without his father. Carol told me that strangely enough she was less afraid of the police than of having to play Kate's love scene, and hoped the arrests would be made before Act Three.

With no economic theatre to which I could transfer, after the Festival guarantee ran out I reluctantly decided that we should have to close on Sunday, which was the last official day of the Festival. To have run on would have involved us in heavy loss, and to ask the cast to play after that date, under threat of imminent arrest *and* for no money, would, I felt, have been asking too much of their overtaxed loyalty. I managed to squeeze my father, who had not been able to come earlier, in on the last night, and he told me that the support he had given me by attending the District Court in his clerical dress had not been misplaced. Sadly enough, he was not to live to hear me legally vindicated a year later.

For a short while after the conclusion of the run I lived in a sort of daze, mechanically going through my military duties. I received a very welcome telegram from the English theatre magazine *Encore*, offering to start a Defence Fund on my behalf. This was subsequently inaugurated by a letter signed by Sean O'Casey, Peter Hall, John Osborne, John Gielgud, Ben W. Levy, Wolf Mankowitz, George Devine and Harold Hobson.

In Dublin, the reactions in theatrical circles and outside were mixed. Quite a large number of people tended to avoid both me and my wife and some quite respectable actors attacked us for 'irresponsibly bringing censorship into the Theatre by putting on this filthy play'. Ordinary citizens tended to shun us in shops and elsewhere. The only place where we seemed to have unqualified support was from the stallholders in the open-air markets of Moore Street. There, my wife would be greeted with cheery cries of 'Up *The Rose Tattoo*' when she was doing her weekly shopping.

A friend and fellow Dublin producer, Jim Fitzgerald, courageously decided to start an Irish fund. He could, however, get no responsible or well-known personages, in or out of the theatre, to lend their name to a carefully worded letter, which was sent to all the papers, but only published in one. Shortly before all these events there had been a big Contempt of Court case in England, and after a scathing judgement, Lord Justice Goddard had fined the American publication, *Newsweek*, a sum amounting to several thousands of pounds. This meant that even the *Irish Times*, which—over the years since the treaty—has moved from a position of Protestant Unionism to that of a sort of Irish *La Prenza*, had to be very careful about any comment printed on the subject of *The Rose Tattoo*. Jim found that quite a number of influential people were prepared to give fairly generously to his Fund, provided he guaranteed them anonymity.

We had a conference with Con and James Heavey to discuss my defence. They decided that because the whole case was so unprecedented and explosive, we should have in court a full complement of defence lawyers. Normally, if one is charged with some minor offence in the District Court, one can safely defend onself, or at most, hire a solicitor for a very small sum. In the case of an indictable offence, appearance in the District Court is only as a prelude to trial by jury or a panel of judges. The purpose of the proceedings is merely to take a summary of the evidence, and the only functions of the District Justice are (a) to see that the prosecution evidence is properly recorded, and (b) *if he considers the prosecution to have produced such feeble evidence that no judge or jury could possibly convict*, to 'refuse informations'. This means, in effect, that he has said that there is no proper evidence of a

case against the accused, and the matter normally goes
no further. This 'refusal of informations' can, in rare
cases be overruled by the Attorney-General. A few
years ago, there was such a case, concerning a man-
slaughter charge arising out of drunken driving. It
was common knowledge that the accused and the
District Justice were on very friendly terms. This was
brought to the attention of the Attorney-General,
and he overruled the District Justice and sent the case
for trial. It is quite normal even in comparatively
serious cases for the defendant to be represented only
by a solicitor at the taking of depositions. In my case,
we felt that, as public interest was so great, it would
be advisable to have the State witnesses cross-ex-
amined at this juncture by expert counsel. Actually,
at that stage, the Attorney-General did intimate
privately to one of my counsel that, should informations be refused, he would, in fact, overrule the District Justice and have the case tried. In the event, however, he thought better of it. For our leader, we
picked on the late Sean Hooper. He was a brilliant
Senior of great charm and had a misleadingly gentle
manner in court.

One night a 'phone call came through from Belfast.
It was George Lodge, the managing director of the
Belfast Opera House. He wanted to know if I would
like to bring *The Rose Tattoo* to Belfast, which was
outside the jurisdiction of the Irish Courts, but incidentally, also outside the area controlled by the
British Lord Chamberlain. I thought carefully before
making up my mind. On the one hand, if I presented
the play there I should be giving the Northern politi-
cians, who are, in fact, anything but liberal in their

outlook, a weapon with which to attack the 'bigotry' of the Republic. Actually, the narrow-mindedness arising from the Northern combination of Low Church Episcopalian and Presbyterian religions is un-equalled anywhere in the world. On the other hand, although the large salary list and expenses involved in travelling, new scenery, etc., would proclude the possibility of profit for myself, I felt I owed it to my actors and actresses to reward their loyalty with further employment at reasonable rates. Also, as a producer, I was naturally anxious to see the play per-formed in a large, well-appointed theatre. So I de-cided that, since any loss of face accruing to my own Government was, under the circumstances, only their just desserts, I would accept the offer.

We had to conduct some rehearsals, in order to substitute Donal Donnelly for Pat Nolan, who was unable to travel and also to adjust the performance to suit a big stage. We rehearsed in the Theatre Royal rehearsal room. Such was our state of mind at the time, that I regarded Louis Elliman's gesture in giving me these facilities as no less than an act of heroism. The dress rehearsal in Belfast was conducted in the presence of officers of the notorious Royal Ulster Constabulary, who laughingly told Mr. Lodge that the play was an entertainment suitable for the Sunday School outing. Although I was, in the circumstances, grateful for their approval, I am inclined to doubt the sincerity of their motivations. An indication of my state of tension at the time, was that I engaged Con Lehane, who is a competent amateur actor, to play one of the small parts in the show, so that he might be on hand if there was any trouble. Military duties prevented me from remaining in Belfast for the run, but my wife told me that among the audience were all the Dublin detectives who had attended Pike. They had been sent at State expense to Belfast in order to corroborate further their evidence.

The play was highly successful in Belfast, a city not noted for its dramatic enthusiasm, and Mr. Lodge told me that, while he had approached us initially for the wrong reasons, he thought it was one of the best shows he had seen in his theatre for some considerable time. His view was shared by a Catholic priest, who was friendly with one of the cast, and who expressed his delight at the performance (having watched it from the wings) by inviting the principals to supper in his presbytery.

On July 4th, the taking of depositions started in the Dublin District Court. As the days went by it became obvious that the State's evidence was to consist largely of a series of detectives and detective sergeants reciting the story of the play in their own words. At no time right up to the conclusion of proceedings a year later did they call any literary or clerical witnesses, or even any of the eight or nine hundred members of the general public who had seen the production. These police witnesses merely slanted the story to make it sound as sordid as possible. Naturally, in the early stages, when public interest was at its height, most of their evidence was transcribed in the newspapers. As the case wore on, public interest decreased, and to this day quite a high percentage of people in Ireland are not aware of the outcome. Thus, in the long run, the Attorney-General succeeded, if not in convicting me, in giving the

general public the impression that I was an un-
desirable character, given to presenting filthy and
sordid plays in my theatre.

Of course, Messrs. Hooper and Heavey were able,
by their skill in cross-examination, to show the police
in a pretty silly light. One of the first witnesses was
Detective Sergeant Martin, who agreed, under cross-
examination, that he had only previously attended
two theatrical performances in twenty years. He also
admitted that on the first occasion when (acting under
instructions) he had visited the play, he had brought
his wife with him. Cross-examination also revealed
that the published copies of the play that were in
police possession, one of which had been submitted in
evidence, were purchased by the State in Duffy's
bookshop. Duffy's specializes in Catholic literature
and religious objects, as well as plays. This published
edition had not then, nor has to this day, incurred the
disapproval of our eagle-eyed Censorship of Publications Board.

From the legal aspect, the case was highly dramatic.
Fairly early in the proceedings, counsel asked Detective Sergeant Martin who had given him his instructions, and how precisely they were framed. At this
point, the prosecution objected, on the grounds that
this contravened a precedent of English Common
Law, that private communications between members
of the police or security forces could not be revealed
in court. This precedent is usually only cited in cases
involving the Secret Service, where revealing of in-
ternal police communications could prejudice public
security. Detective Sergeant Wedick had apparently
submitted a report on the play to his superiors. Mr.

15. The warm welcome outside the court.

16. Brendan Behan, Dublin, 1960.

Hooper seemed to have reason to believe that this report was not unfavourable to the production. This would not have surprised me, as in court he appeared rather more sophisticated than his colleagues. At any rate, when Mr. Hooper asked that this report should be produced, the prosecution again objected on the same grounds as before. After some legal discussion, District Justice Flynn agreed to 'state a case' to the High Court on the point. This, in effect, meant that the legal arguments on the question of police privilege would be submitted to three judges in the High Court, who would give a ruling as to their rights in the matter. Should they rule against us we should have to bear the heavy costs of such a hearing. With these points left in abeyance the police continued with their evidence.

Many weeks later the High Court sat to decide this knotty problem. To our horror they decided against me. Con rang me in barracks with the news. There were two alternatives open to us. One was to appeal the High Court decision to the Supreme Court, and the other to accept the ruling and the costs (which amounted to several thousand pounds). After consulting with my wife, I decided that things could not be much worse, and that I should be ruined anyway, whatever the outcome in the District Court. It was really a gambler's decision of Double or Quits. So I felt I had better tell Con to appeal.

Further time passed and the Supreme Court, consisting of five judges this time, considered the problem. With a cunning judgement worthy of King Solomon and the Baby, they decided that the District Justice had had no legal authority to submit such a question in the first place, but that he was bound to decide the matter himself. This decision meant that the High Court proceedings were invalidated and the State would have to pay the costs. The Supreme Court also decided to charge only one day of their five-day session against me. The remainder was to be a liability of the prosecution. By this time, the tax-payer had had to foot an enormous bill for legal costs, as well as the expenses incurred in the police trip to Belfast, and the indirect expenses involved in their endless appearances in court.

In June 1958, just a year after it had started, the taking of depositions was concluded. District Justice Flynn, in a summing-up worthy of a much higher court, ruled that the State had presented him with no evidence of my having presented 'an indecent performance'. Incidentally, the word 'profane' had been dropped from the charge fairly early on. He paid tribute to the sincerity of the individual police officers involved, but commented, 'I can only infer that by arresting the accused, the object would be achieved of closing down the play. But surely if that were the object, nothing could be more devastating than to restrain the production before even a hearing is held. It smacks to me of the frontier principle, "Shoot first, and talk after".'

I walked out of the court, as they say, a free man; but what have been the consequences? The Pike had, not unnaturally, been completely disorganized by the affair. The membership had dropped from a figure of three thousand to three hundred. All during the period of the case, I had, for obvious reasons, to avoid the presentation of any play which could possibly be considered even faintly controversial. Although the various Funds had covered the monies required for the immediate conduct of the defence, I was in considerable debt to my lawyers. The mental strain of the proceedings was so great that at one stage I developed a rash, diagnosed as one common to victims of the blitz.

Friends have complimented me on my courage in taking the stand I did, but looking back on the events I have recorded, it doesn't seem to me that I ever had any reasonable alternative to the course I took. If, at the beginning, I had taken off the play, it would have been tantamount to a public admission of guilt; as would have been my giving of an undertaking not to proceed with the performances after my arrest. My decision to continue with the appeal to the Supreme Court was dictated by the knowledge that I should be completely bankrupt anyway, if I had accepted the High Court decision.

While the case was still *sub judice*, there was another episode which underlines the difficulties of theatrical presentation in Ireland. As I remarked in the previous chapter, there has been a tendency in post-war Ireland to involve the Church in all sorts of matters, not really its concern. In this, the over-enthusiastic sections of the laity are as much, if not more to blame than the clergy. Some misguided minor official was foolish enough to invite the Archbishop of Dublin, Dr. McQuade, an austere former headmaster of Blackrock College (affectionately known throughout the city as John Charles) to celebrate a Votive Mass to mark the opening of the Festival. This put the Archbishop in an impossible position, as he was being

asked to give religious blessing to works by Sean
O'Casey and James Joyce. Now, Sean O'Casey,
however great a dramatist and sincere a man, has
devoted his fiery talents for a large number of years to
the denigration of the Irish priesthood and the support of Communism. James Joyce, as I explained
earlier, has been for a long time the devilish *bête noire*
of Irish Catholicism. Even for the most jovial of pre-
lates, this would have been asking a bit much, whatever his admiration for the artistic merits of the two
authors.

John Charles who, at the best of times, tends to
regard the Dublin diocese as an extension of his
academic life, with his parish priests as the masters,
his curates as the prefects, and the laity as his recalci-
trant pupils, sent letters to the Festival Council and
the trade unions, querying the intention of the organizers to present plays of 'an objectionable nature'.
A big row blew up. The Tourist Board, bound under
its constitution to refrain from engaging in controversial matters, withdrew its financial support from
the scheme, and the whole Festival had to be aban-
doned. Subsequently, after much delicate negotiation
between the Board, Brendan Smith, the organizer,
and Michael Killanin, the chairman, it has been revived, and after three successful and comparatively
uneventful repetitions, looks like becoming a respected annual event. Nowadays, of course, no Votive
Mass is celebrated or expected.

As a gesture of disapproval at the dropping of his
own and Joyce's plays from the ill-fated Festival, Sean
O'Casey has consistently refused to allow any of his
work to be performed in his native city. This has

meant severe loss of income to the Abbey Theatre, which relied on revivals of his earlier works as money-spinners. Sam Beckett too joined in, with a bann, now lifted, on the performance of his works in Dublin, as a gesture of sympathy for his late friend, James Joyce.

Chapter VI

LOOKING FORWARD

~~~~~~

'SORRY ABOUT ALL YOUR TROUBLE over *The Rose Tattoo*. Bastards, bastards, . . .' wrote Sam Beckett to me in August 1957.

Up to the 1950's the two playwrights who did most to spread the fame of the Irish Theatre throughout the world, were Synge and O'Casey. In the prose field, Joyce, and in more recent years, Sean O'Faoilain, and Frank O'Connor, are the most highly thought of in international literary circles. All these five writers have called down on their heads the abuse of the Irish middle-class moralists. In the case of O'Casey and Synge, this was manifested in riots at the first performances of some of their plays, and in the others, by the activities of the Censorship of Publications Board.

In the last five years it is Samuel Beckett and Brendan Behan who have directed the attention of foreign critics to Irish writing. Times have changed, for *The Hostage*, which in many ways is far more outspoken than any of the works of O'Casey that have been performed in Dublin, had a comparatively uneventful presentation there, except for an organized walk-out about three-quarters of the way through the run, and some fairly sharp newspaper criticisms. Actually, the contrast between the English critics and the Dublin ones is rather startling. To give the reader some indication of this, I quote from the *Irish Independent*, the *Irish Times*, and then from what I suppose is the best of the London notices, written in the *Sunday Times* by Harold Hobson:

'In the low-class Dublin lodging house in which it is set, an improbable group of characters sing parodies, talk a great deal and do some vaudeville dance routines which frequently erupt into scenes of uninhibited and undisciplined abandon.

Those who go to the theatre to see a story unfolded in the conventional manner will find *The Hostage* disappointing.

There is a plot, one which has been used many times by authors over the past forty years. A young British soldier has been captured in a border raid and is being held as hostage for a Republican prisoner under sentence of death in Belfast. But the time allotted to its development and solution is a tiny fraction of the running time. The rest is music-hall.

There is a surfeit of the type of tasteless gibe one would expect from third-rate comedians, and many of the worn-out jokes were not amusing even at first hearing. The serious content is almost lost under an avalanche of bawdiness and irrelevancies, and it is a tribute to Mr. Behan's sense of the theatre that the thread of pathos and of protest against the useless taking of young lives is not completely snowed under.'   *Irish Independent*

'. . . but the over-all impression when the final curtain had fallen was one of disappointment. Maybe because there had been too many preliminary fanfares . . . maybe because O'Casey used to do the same sort of thing more effectively, because he knew the value of economy. . . .'   *Irish Times*

'A masterpiece should have magnaminity and Mr. Behan's portrait of the young English soldier is magnanimous indeed. Above all it should have life and should have it more abundantly. Life is what *The Hostage* is rich in. It shouts, sings, thunders and stamps with life. And when the life of the unself-pitying English orphan is over, Mr. Behan finds for him an epitaph that is classically restrained and beautiful.

A girl drops on her knee beside the accidentally shot body and stills the boisterous tumult of this joyous, rowdy play with words of staggering simplicity. "He died in a foreign country and at home he had no-one." Nothing finer in this kind has been written for two thousand years, nothing since. . . .

> Ante diem periet:
> Sed miles sed pro patria.

The Irish, the Southern Irish, the I.R.A. Irish have found in Mr. Behan a dramatist in the line of Mr. O'Casey. They should treasure him and be proud of him.'

Sunday Times

From the remarks quoted at the beginning of the chapter, and from various things he has said to me from time to time, I know that Sam Beckett feels as strongly about the moronic element of his fellow-countrymen as do the others. But this has not revealed itself in his writing, nor has he at any time drawn on himself the opprobium of his compatriots at home. By leaving Ireland for France as a young man, he cut himself off, both consciously and subconsciously from the Irish way of life and happenings in Ireland. Unlike Sean O'Casey, who from his recent writings and pronouncements, obviously is a regular reader of Irish newspapers of every shade of opinion, Beckett has

kept as few ties as possible with the land of his birth.
The fact that he has been talking, thinking and writing
in French has increased his isolation from Irish affairs.
In fact, I am convinced that it is only his friendship
with Joyce and Joyce's bitterness against Ireland that
has made Beckett even conscious of the Irish sex-
religion neurosis.

Sam Beckett has dallied with various philosophical
outlooks during his life. That his conclusions on
spiritual matters are indeterminate, I think is obvious
from his more recent writing. There is no doubt,
however, that his writing is so detached that the
Catholic, or indeed any Christian, ethic could be fitted into the framework of—say—*Waiting for Godot*
by any nimble theologian, if he so wished. But Sam
is far too deep and subtle a writer to allow any personal feelings, such as his sympathy with Joyce, to
colour the finished product in any way. In the Dublin
reviews of *Godot* the nearest approach to a realization
that Beckett might not subscribe to the orthodox
Irish Catholic view of life was the vague unease of
Ita Mallin in the *Irish Independent*. She neatly sum-
marized her feelings by saying, 'We are too positive
here perhaps, in our spiritual beliefs and disbeliefs, to
be provoked into vague and tenuous theorizing.'

Brendan's views of life and Ireland are not unlike
those of Sean O'Casey, of whom he is a great ad-
mirer. But there are two important differences between them although their backgrounds, in the eyes
of the outside world, must seem much the same.
O'Casey's father was a militant Protestant, whose dislike of Catholicism far outweighed his love of Ireland.
Because of this, although unlike many of his co-

religionists, O'Casey passed through a phase of violent nationalism, and consequently had no pro-British bias, his anti-Catholicism is tinged slightly and I am sure subconsciously with Orangism. In theory, to judge from his subsequent writings and public statements, he has since moved from national-ist republicanism to international atheist commun-ism. Nevertheless, his anti-clerical jeerings have a Protestant rather than an atheist slant. This, in some subtle way, makes them even more offensive to many Irishmen than straightforward atheism. His atheism, in fact, strikes me as being of a superficial nature; one might almost say adopted purely for the sake of annoying the Irish clergy.

Brendan was brought up as a Catholic, and while his approach to that faith could hardly be called orthodox, any actual or implied criticisms of the clergy or the 'way out' aspects of Catholic nationalism comes, as it were, from a Catholic-based firing point. In fact, many of the preposterous and outrageous things he says in *The Hostage* are merely a reflection of the outlook of the more outspoken Dublin work-ing-class pub customers.

The other great difference between himself and O'Casey is that Brendan had a much happier child-hood. The Behan family started life in a Dublin slum, not far from where O'Casey's own childhood was spent, but they were moved while Brendan was still at school to the healthier atmosphere of Crumlin. Also, Brendan's grandmother saw to it that the children got enough food and clothing during Stephen's periods of unemployment.

O'Casey had the misfortune to be the last of a

family of thirteen, eight of whom died in infancy as a direct result of the filth and degradation of the conditions under which they lived. A chronic eye disease, caused by the filthy conditions which had killed his brothers and sisters, made him partially blind from early childhood. As a young man he was one of James Larkin's assistants at the bitterest period of Irish Labour history, namely the 1913 Lock-Out. The support given by certain of the clergy to the employers left an indelible impression on his Protestant mind.

Stephen Behan, on the other hand, was at the time employed by a small contractor in painting a chapel at the Curragh Camp. As a painter, he was an artisan. It was the labourers of the larger Dublin contractors and the transport workers who were so deeply affected by the hatreds at this time. Also, it is quite obvious to anyone who knows the Behan family that they have a jollity of spirit capable of rising above any adversity in which they find themselves.

As a youth, Brendan's outlook on religion and politics in Dublin would, to a certain extent, have been coloured by the Larkin tradition, which even today is strong in the city's proletariat, and secures Young Jim's parliamentary seat at the present time. But Brendan is of a different generation and could not be expected to feel so strongly on the issues which are still so very much a part of O'Casey's motivating force.

Sam Beckett was brought up in a comfortable professional home and a Protestant boarding school. The Civil War was over by the time he was twenty and he would have been almost completely unaffected by the religious and political tensions of his native city. His disapproval of modern Ireland is therefore entirely as a result of his friendship with Joyce and the natural abhorrence of a scholar and man of letters at the intrusion of politics and religion into cultural matters. However, despite the fact that he is so remote from Dublin today, he has shown a marked tendency in his more recent writings to make almost exclusive use of the rhythms of Dublinese in his dramatic dialogue. Recently, he has translated *La Manivelle*, a radio play by the French writer, Robert Pinget, into English, and his translation, together with the French original, is presented by his Paris publishers *Les Editions de Minuit* in the one volume. As an illustration of the close similarity between his interpretation of the French dialogue and Brendan Behan's dialogue, I quote the following three extracts. The first is the French dialogue of Pinget, which in itself is interesting in that it demonstrates the basic affinity between the atmospheres of Ireland and France. The second is Sam's translation of the same passage, and the third, a section of Act One of *The Quare Fellow*.

POMMARD Hélène, Hélène Jumeau jolie fille, elle aurait mon age, elle était de 83.

TOUPIN Et Rose Boulette, la belle Rose, elle est bien mince aujourd'hui, et Françoise Loin, et Renée comment donc, Renée, Renée, Renée Bottu voilà, est-ce qu'elle n' avait pas épousé un Sancou.

POMMARD Son frère, son frère Alfred avait épousé Corine Sancou, Légère légère la Corine souvenez-vous.

TOUPIN Pensez si je me souviens, Corine Sancou, elle

levait bien la cuisse nom de sort, ha ha ha la cuisse nom de sort.

POMMARD   Sacré Toupin, Sacré Toupin.

      BRUIT DE VOITURE

TOUPIN   Et Louisette Pilochat, en voilà une qui a bien mal fini.

POMMARD   La fille à Jean-Pierre parfaitement, les parents étaient bien responsables croyez-moi.

*   *   *

CREAM   Helen, Helen Bliss, pretty girl, she'd be my age, 83 saw the light of day.

GORMAN   And Rosie Plumpton bonny Rosie staring up at the lid these thirty years she must be now and Molly Berry and Eva what was her name Eva Hart that's right Eva Hart didn't she marry a Crumplin.

CREAM   Her brother, her brother Alfred married Gertie Crumplin great one for the lads she was you remember, Gertie great one for the lads.

GORMAN   Do I remember, Gertie Crumplin great bit of skirt by God, hee hee hee great bit of skirt.

CREAM   You old dog you!

      Roar of Engine.

GORMAN   And Nelly Crowther there's one came to a nasty end.

CREAM   Simon's daughter that's right, the parents were greatly to blame you can take it from me.

*   *   *

NEIGHBOUR   Meena la Bloom, do you remember her?

DUNLAVIN   Indeed and I do; many's the seaman myself and Meena gave the hey and a do, and Mickey Finn to.

NEIGHBOUR   And poor May Oblong.

DUNLAVIN   Ah, where do you leave poor May? . . .

NEIGHBOUR   Ah, poor May, God help her, she was the heart of the roll . . .

And will you ever forget poor Lottie L'Estrange, that got had up for pushing the soldier into Spencer Dock?

DUNLAVIN   Ah, God be with the youth of us.

NEIGHBOUR   And Cork Annie, and Lady Limerick.

DUNLAVIN   And Julia Rice and the Goofy One.

If Beckett continues this trend, it is going to raise problems regarding the production of his work in England. There are, at most, half a dozen Irish actors and actresses well known on the London stage, and of these, the only one whose stature with the public is comparable to that of the knights and dames of the theatrical establishment is Siobhan McKenna. The same, as far as I can judge, is true of New York. There has been a tendency in the last few years for London audiences to accept exciting new plays without the use of such established stars. But when this has happened, it has been as a result of patient work over a period of time to build up the reputation of a theatrical organization such as the English Stage Company or Theatre Workshop. In such cases the theatre, or perhaps, in the case of Littlewood, the producer, takes the place of the star in the mind of the public.

A London audience will accept a play in Cockney dialect, because they understand it. If the individual member of the audience does not speak like a Cockney himself, because he hears this dialect spoken in the street around him he understands it and finds pleasure and amusement in the natural playing with words which is part of the attraction of strong dialect.

A number of North Country plays have been very successful in London recently, and it is significant that the young star to have made the biggest impact on English theatre in 1960–1 is Albert Finney, himself a North Country man. I think the reason for this easy acceptance of the North Country dialect is the long tradition of North Country humour in the British music-hall—which, over recent years, has been continued in the new media of radio and television.

With Irish dialect, the public reaction in England is quite different. There has been no appreciable traffic from Ireland in radio or films, as there has, for instance, with the United States. The constant flow of films from America has built up in Britain an understanding of American dialects and humour. This flow, in the first instance, had its origins in economics. The huge population of the United States made it possible for Hollywood producers to recover their costs on any film from its American distribution. This has meant that over the last thirty years, American film companies have been able to build up an appreciation of American dialect and humour in Britain at no financial risk, and over recent years, both radio and television have been affected in the same way.

The differences of speech and custom between Ireland and Britain are certainly no greater than those between Britain and the United States. But there has been no economic weapon with which to fight for a place in the British entertainment market. It is possible that the sensational build up of Beckett's reputation, which was started by *Waiting for Godot* will be sufficiently strong to overcome the handicap of Irish dialect, should he see fit to use it in his future plays. I have already commented on the press reaction to the playing of Estragon and Vladimir as Irish. It was significant that in the television production Donald McWhinnie chose not to allow Jack McGowran, who played Vladimir, to speak in his natural Dublinese. I discussed the matter with McGowran and he told me that he was in complete agreement with the producer, in thinking that British television viewers might be confused and prejudiced by the dialect.

The difficulties of presenting a play, the theme and dialogue of which are purely Irish, was underlined for me by my production of Dominic Behan's *Posterity be Damned* in the Metropolitan Theatre, Edgeware Road, in April 1960. Taken strictly as a play, it had many good qualities, although, in common with a number of highly successful hits, it also contained many faults. Its theme, however, unlike those of his elder brother, was strictly concerned with Irish matters. Dominic's thesis, expressed in a ballad running through the production, was that the time for *dying* for Ireland had passed and that the youth of the country should now be taught to *live* and work for better social conditions in the Ireland of the future.

When the piece was presented in Dublin it played to very good business and, had theatrical conditions permitted, would have enjoyed a long run. In London, the publicity potential of presenting a play by Brendan's brother, while *The Hostage* was still packing a West End theatre, was enormous, and the Granada organization, of which the Metropolitan is a part, exploited it to the full. The play was set in a pub, and it was written by a Behan. I felt it was with some reluctance that the management removed the huge leprechaun accompanying the slogan 'London's Irish Music-Hall' which plastered the front of the theatre before our arrival.

At the Press conference, draught Guinness and Irish whiskey flowed like water, and a few days afterwards, brother Brendan and the Behan parents put in an appearance at a rehearsal, accompanied by Brendan's usual entourage of newsmen. Soon they had him in the 'Running Horse' across the road from the theatre, and his lunch was strictly of a liquid nature. One of the journalists, who on the particular occasion, I noticed trying to prevent his colleagues from exploiting Brendan's weakness to their own advantage was the Jewish drama critic of the *Daily Herald*, David Nathan. Brendan has a very high regard for anybody Jewish, and of my particular circle the two people who seemed to be able to do most to control his wilder exuberances were, in the McDaid's days, Beverley McNamara, and subsequently my wife, Carol, both of whom are Jewish.

In America, his 'protector' in New York was Jewish columnist Leonard Lyons, who has quoted one of Brendan's most famous quips on the subject. 'The Hebrews and the Gaels have much in common. Both are exotic enough to be interesting and not foreign enough to be alarming.' Brendan is also quoted as having said, 'The Irish and the Jews hate each other royally, you know; but in this Protestant world we had better stick together.'

Egged on by the journalists and stimulated by the alcoholic atmosphere, the two brothers then had the row referred to in Chapter Two. The cumulative effect of all this was that we had one of the most extraordinary first nights that must ever have been witnessed in a London theatre. The audience was divided into three distinct parts. One, respectable, disapproving English, another, exuberant and enthusiastic Irish, the third, exuberant and disapproving Irish. The latter gave loud vent to their disagreement with the political implications of the play, and also to their rejection of the suggestion that (in view of the pub setting and the behaviour of many of the characters) the Irish were a nation of drunks and blasphemers. They did not make their point very well, however, for one man reeled out of the Circle bar, which was packed throughout the evening, shouting, 'Why do you always show the Irish as a crowd of drunks?' and another, 'Ah, for Jazes sake, will you cut out the blasphemy!'

All this furore must have made it very difficult for any serious theatre-goer to judge the play on its merits. Also, the author, who was not unnaturally made very nervous by the colossal publicity build-up, had himself steadied his nerves to such an extent that he ruined his own rendering of the play's thematic ballad. Later in the run, however, when things had settled down, I formed the impression that, despite the more favourable circumstances, the non-Irish patrons found both theme and dialogue rather difficult to follow.

In the recent London presentation of *The Playboy of the Western World* I am told that many of the audience had difficulty in following the dialogue, although the play is an accepted classic and would have been read by many of them. The production had been mounted in Dublin for the 1960 Theatre Festival and had in the cast the cream of the Irish acting profession, headed by Siobnan McKenna, Donal Donnelly and Eithne Dunne. No doubt the presence of Miss McKenna contributed largely to the financial success of the venture, which was the first genuinely all-Irish presentation to be universally acclaimed in London for a long time. For the reasons already mentioned, however, it seems very difficult in the ordinary way to provide an authentic Irish atmosphere, dialect and theme, which can be fully appreciated by a non-Irish English-speaking audience. The producer who succeeds in achieving this will perform a great service to Irish playwriting and to his country's reputation abroad.

From what I know of him, Samuel Beckett will continue to write in his own particular and peculiar way whatever seems best to him. He will remain in Paris and will continue to be unaffected by any influences other than those which are locked in his subconscious. If his writing becomes more Irish, it will be because as a man gets older, the memories of his youth become stronger. He will never return to Ireland for any length of time, and even if he were to, his cultivated detachment would prevent his becoming involved in any way in Irish affairs.

What of Brendan Behan? Not unnaturally, he was invited to New York for the *première* of *The Hostage* at the Cort Theatre. Prior to this, he had been considerably built up as a personality in the American Press, which had given large coverage to his exploits in London during the runs of *The Quare Fellow* and

The Hostage. This build up climaxed in his appearance, again in a semi-comitose state on the Ed Murrow international television hook-up *It's a Small World*, which was recorded in Dublin shortly before his departure. The American public, with its respect for all things televisual, was almost awed at the thought of anyone behaving so outrageously on one of its top programmes. Scott Fitzgerald and, more recently, Dylan Thomas, had whetted its appetite for self-destructive genius, and Brendan's arrival in the States was as eagerly awaited as any film star's.

The management of *The Hostage* booked him into the Algonquin, which is a famous, old-fashioned hotel, much patronized by well-known writers and directors who have a sort of unofficial club there. After big first nights, it is crowded with celebrities, who engage in brilliant conversation, as far as I can gather, much in the manner of the patrons of the Café Royal in Oscar Wilde's time. Brendan, with his throaty Dublin voice and rich language, exploded like a bomb in this brittle, wisecracking society. As long as I have known him, he has found a perverse delight in shattering carefully nurtured atmospheres. Actually, the number of four-letter words per hundred in his normal speech is not very much higher than that of the building worker in the natural habitat of job or pub. But because he is a Behan, he uses such words with greater imagination than his comrades, and because he is Brendan, he has never modified his speech to suit his company.

I will never forget the effect he created at a garden party during the first Theatre Festival. This was to be held in the grounds of the Royal Marine Hotel, Dun

Laoghaire, but rain had driven the guests, who included diplomats, high society, and visiting theatrical notabilities, into the public rooms of the hotel itself. I met Brendan in the densely crowded foyer. I had just been talking to Siobhan O'Casey, daughter of the playwright, and wishing to make polite conversation with Brendan, I asked him if he had met her, remarking that she was a very nice girl. 'Certainly I met her,' he bellowed, 'and why wouldn't she be a nice girl? She's a f——ing Communist like her father!' I digested this and searched for a witty reply. By the time I had found one, I noticed Brendan and I were completely alone in the large hall.

During this first visit to America he was still completely on the wagon, and he was secured by comedian, Jack Paar, for regular appearances on his television programme. I believe that Paar is brilliant at putting people at their ease, and succeeded in getting a number of relaxed and witty interviews from Brendan, without any recourse to the bottle. During the run at The Cort, he was reported to have arrived at the theatre in a drunken state and created a great disturbance in his traditional manner. I formed the opinion, reading the reports of this outburst in Dublin, that it was a phoney one, organized by the publicity boys to stimulate business, which had apparently been dropping off a little. After this, he returned to Dublin, and was supposed to be getting on with his new play, until Joan Littlewood arrived to put pressure on him to finish it, when he disintegrated into a further bout of drunkenness.

For her, this must have been a great disappointment and may have been a contributory factor to her decision, announced as I write, to quit the English theatre for an extended period. It was *The Quare Fellow* which first drew serious public and critical attention to the fine work she had been doing in the Theatre Royal, Stratford East, and previously in the north of England. My wife can distinctly remember how, around about 1946, when working as secretary to the theatrical manager of the British Council in London, she was told to go and get rid of some crank who was making a nuisance of herself in the outer office. The 'crank' was Joan Littlewood. Fourteen years later, this same 'crank' had four separate productions running simultaneously in the West End of London. There is no doubt in my mind that Brendan's widely publicized antics played a very important part in this remarkable transition.

Joan has no use for the polite toadying and patronage-seeking tactics of many of the more important personages of the English theatre. Her uncompromising Left Wing opinions make her anathema to the British Establishment. In the ordinary way, she could have been turning out a continuous flow of superb productions over a period of many years before the most important West Fnd impresarios would have taken the trouble to appraise her work.

Before the arrival of Brendan in Stratford East, she had had outspoken support from only a very few of the English critics, and the selection of Theatre Workshop as representative of Britain at the Paris International Theatre Festival brought a howl of protest both from the entrenched sections of the theatrical profession and the stodgier newspapers. Although *The Quare Fellow* was not, I believe, a financial success in the West End, it sharply focused attention on activities in Angel Lane. When *The Hostage*, *A Taste of Honey*, *Make me an Offer*, *Fings Ain't Wot They Used T' Be*, and other plays were *premièred* in Stratford East, which is half an hour on the Underground from central London, Britain's leading critics were there in as full a force as if the theatre had been located in Shaftesbury Avenue. This great wave of popularity rather overloaded the organizational resources of the theatre, and was a constant drain on Joan's reserve of actors, built up over the years and trained in her own unusual methods.

There were other reasons for her phenomenal success, apart from Brendan on the one hand and her fine productions on the other. Since the end of World War II and the period of the Labour Government, there has been taking place an imperceptible social revolution. People with non-public school accents have been finding themselves in positions of power in business and industry, and the artisan class, in particular, has found itself in possession of a lot more money than the lower ranks of white-collar workers. This has meant that public attention has been focused on drama which has as its background places outside the drawing-room. Consequently, as the only theatre completely devoted to working-class drama, Theatre Workshop was bound to benefit.

There is also a third reason, which explains the success particularly of *A Taste of Honey* and *Fings Ain't Wot They Used T' Be*. This is the enormous interest of post-war Britain in vice and sex. The English are, on the whole, an inhibited people. They have a basic prudery and gaucheness in sex matters which

185

sets them apart from almost every other nation in Europe. One of the reasons, in fact, for the peculiar sex neurosis of the Irish people today is that the Irish have adopted the English sex prudery which is not, in fact, natural to them. In England, the realization that many of the restraints and taboos of Victorian times are unnatural and even psychologically harmful, combined with the decline of organized religion has led to a considerable laxity in sex matters, particularly since World War II. This, in turn, has brought about a morbid interest in vice and low life. *A Taste of Honey* is, in my opinion, one of the best and most moving of post-war English plays, but I am quite sure that the thing that turned it from an artistic to a big popular success was the fact that the heroine is involved, first with a Negro sailor and then with a homosexual. The setting of *The Hostage* in a brothel must have helped the box-office. In Frank Dermody's original Irish language production, there was not nearly so much emphasis on the nature of the establishment, and in fact the character of Princess Grace materialized somewhere between St. Stephen's Green and Angel Lane.

How Joan Littlewood will succeed in achieving her artistic aims while at the same time retaining the popularity which is essential to the financial security of her theatre remains to be seen. At the moment, it looks extremely unlikely that *Richard's Cork Leg* will ever entertain the audiences of Stratford East, or indeed, I am sorry to say, any other audiences.

As soon as things had quietened down in Dublin, Brendan set off again for the United States; this time, it was reported, to appear as master of ceremonies in a

cabaret-type revue. His lapse during Joan Littlewood's visit seems to have undermined his determination to keep teetotal and soon the reports
started pouring in of drunken episodes in every part
of the continent. It sounds as if he was particularly
unfortunate in Canada, where he was initially invited
to address a University society. Leonard Lyons, who
continued to take an interest in Brendan and tried to
look after him as far as possible, reported in *The
Lyon's Den* on 11th December 1960:

'. . . the 'phone operator said that Brendan Behan was
calling from Montreal. Another man came on first and
said how tragic it was, about the author of *The Hostage*.
Friday was a church holiday in Montreal, and all the bars
were closed. But some reporters, he said, took Behan to the
Press Club where a bar was open, and goaded him into
drinking, for a story.

  ' "Hello. How are you?" Behan began, his voice rising
and falling in pain and pleasure. His favourite 4-Letter
word punctuated his talk. "I'm —— lousy, —— lousy. I'm
—— drunk and I'm not even —— happy. I wish to Jayzuz
I hadn't left New York. Why in the name of Jayzuz don't
you rescue me? I'm hell-holed in this —— place. I wish I'd
never come here. New York's the only place on this continent where you have an excuse for being."

  'He'd gone to Montreal to lecture, but felt lost in the hin-
terlands. He had defined a city as "a place where you're least
likely to be bitten by a wild ass." Now he moaned, 'Save me.'

  'I wish there were some way I could rescue Behan—not
from Montreal, but from the mad compulsion and from
the cruel ones who spike his soft drinks. He had overcome
the sickness in New York, where the fact that he is a man
of rare talent and a true free spirit made the city open its
doors to him. We'd been together in many places here, in

sawdust bars and elegant rooms, and everyone felt brightened by his wit and innate warmth.

'Drinks were being served everywhere I took him, but he never touched a drop. He recently came to my son's Bar Mitzvah, where the drinks flowed freely but he shunned them all. Yesterday Bill Mark sent me the photos of that event—of the traditional *horah* we all danced—and, in the center, was the sober Behan, wearing a *yarmulka*, dancing like an Irish king.'

The reports of his activities continued to come in. One that caused considerable consternation in Europe was from Hollywood. It was to the effect that some well-known film producer or company had purchased the film rights of his first play, *The Quare Fellow*. When Brendan is drunk he has an unfortunate habit of selling his work several times over to different managements. During the first London production of *The Quare Fellow*, the rights of which had been very carefully sewn up by Jerry Raffles for Theatre Workshop, among the audience was the French-American patron of the arts, Jacqueline Sundstrom. She was very deeply impressed with the play and the next day she called her solicitor and instructed him to take an option on it for the film and French stage rights. A few days after the necessary arrangements had been made and the contract signed, Sam Spiegel of Columbia got hold of Brendan and paid him two hundred pounds for an option on the film rights. This, when it was discovered, caused considerable upset all round, and it wasn't sorted out until the courts a year later decided in Mrs. Sundstrom's favour. So naturally, in this autumn of 1961, all those who have brought *The Quare Fellow* film to a fairly advanced state of preparation are thrown into a panic any time Brendan, in his cups, is reported or misreported in such a way as to suggest that this sort of thing could happen again.

Not long ago, J. B. Priestley, writing in the *Sunday Times*, said, 'The man—he is usually a director not primarily a writer—who can compel the film industry to serve his purpose will probably have few ideas but uncommon tenacity. He has to hold a dream in an iron grasp. He must carry his idea, still fresh and untainted, through months, perhaps years, of discussions, arguments, challenges and ultimatums, as if he had sworn to bring a nosegay through ten cavalry charges and a peace conference.'

I would not say that Jacqueline Sundstrom has few ideas, but she certainly has uncommon tenacity. She was born in France, but adopted by wealthy Americans and brought up in the United States. She disliked life there and returned to France, a rich woman feeling a need to use her money for the benefit of others. She would visit the little theatres in Paris and London, wherever new writers and directors were working, and where she found talent she would give assistance, financial and otherwise, sometimes so indirectly that the recipients were not even aware of who their benefactress was. She was a writer for M.C.A. for a time, which probably accounts for the keenness of her literary eye.

Having had her *Quare Fellow* rights confirmed by the courts, her first move was to get it put on in Paris. She got it translated by Boris Vian. Boris Vian, who died shortly after the play was put on, was one of the most remarkable people in the world of the Left

Bank. Trained as an engineer, he became famous as a jazz trumpeter and was the man really responsible for starting the craze for cellar jazz clubs in Paris. He wrote a number of very fine novels and plays, but became notorious for writing a book which he subsequently turned into a film, called *J'irai cracher sur votre tombe*, which he wrote under the name of Vernon Sullivan, purporting it to be a translation of an American novel. The work was highly sensational and he was accused in a court case of pornography.

The translation of *The Quare Fellow*, under the brilliant French title of *Le Client du Matin* was very good indeed. It was presented in the Theatre de l'Oeuvre in April 1959, directed by Georges Wilson of the T.N.P. Unfortunately, despite an excellent press, it did not have a very long run, although Brendan, as always, made a big impact with Parisian newspapermen. Mrs. Sundstrom tried to interest various people in making the film, but it wasn't until some years later, when she was working as dialogue writer on a film he was producing in Holland, that she met the American director, Arthur Dreifus. Dreifus was the first person she could get to take the project seriously.

One of the problems of *The Quare Fellow* as a film is that there is no really central character, with whom the audience can identify itself. In my own production of the play, Warder Regan definitely comes out as this, but it is thought by the film people that he would not be a suitable central figure. The only other part which comes out as important in the stage version is that of Dunlavin, and again he is not considered as acceptable. Despite the fact that a Hollywood drama critic in New York described the play as 'one of the greatest documents of all time' when it was directed by Jose Quintero in the Greenwich Village 'Circle in the Square' Theatre, none of the commercial film companies would even consider it. Sam Spiegel, during his unfortunate period of interest in the work, is said to have remarked, 'Of course *The Quare Fellow* has to be seen, otherwise the whole thing is impossible . . . there is no leading man.'

After various treatments and screenplays had been tried, Arthur decided to write his own screenplay. This he has done and in it he has made Warder Cremin, the young Irish-speaking newcomer to the prison, the central figure. This certainly would seem to have some prospects of success, as Cremin, although a fairly small part in the original, is undoubtedly the most sympathetic character in the play from the point of view of the average audience, and as a newcomer to the job, most of the explanations of the grizzly routine of execution are made to him.

To satisfy the film financiers, Mr Dreifus has had to introduce a feminine interest into the story. This he has done by having Cremin form an attachment to the wife of the condemned man, whom he meets in his lodgings, where she is awaiting news of a reprieve. To me, this seems an unfortunate complication, as apart from any other consideration, it is bound to affect the claustrophobic atmosphere of having the whole action take place, as it does in the play, inside the prison. But after so many years of unsuccessful attempts to finance the film, Mrs. Sundstrom and Mr. Dreifus are not really in a position to argue further with the moguls. At any rate, as Brecht is said to have frequently remarked, 'The proof of the pudding is in the eating,' and I am glad to say that if all goes well, the film should be completed at Ardmore Studios, County Wicklow, before the summer of 1962, eight years after I first presented it in Dublin.

I have already said that I am sure Sam Beckett will go on writing in his own unorthodox, disciplined way. I wish I could say the same for Brendan. There are signs that, unlike Sean O'Casey, he intends to remain firmly attached to his roots in Dublin. Of course, his exploits in the United States have made him extremely unpopular in certain quarters at home. One of his chief critics is, curiously enough, Dublin's first and only Jewish Lord Mayor, Robert Briscoe. Briscoe himself made an extremely successful goodwill tour of the States some years ago and did a lot to demolish the traditional picture of the drunken stage Irishman begorrahing his way from bar to bar and from fight to fight. The reason for his bitterness against Brendan is probably that he feels that he is undoing, by his boozy antics, all his own efforts to break down this picture.

Ireland's position relative to England has given us a bit of an inferiority complex, but I think that the time has come to be a little less self-conscious. Like any new small country, we have our problems and our faults. But our record of progress in matters of industry and social organization is quite a good one for a mere forty years of self-government, particularly when you consider the extraordinary conditions prevailing in the country in 1921, and the unfortunate fact of the severing of the industrial north. Our record abroad, particularly in the field of United Nations affairs has been extremely good, and as a nation we are at the moment very popular with all the other small new countries in the world. The fact that the President of the General Assembly of the United Nations is an Irish civil servant, and their former military commander in Africa is a product of our own military training system is surely evidence enough of the respect accorded to us abroad. I think, therefore, that we can afford to look leniently on Brendan's shenanigans. His literary output is another matter. If he stays at home he will remain in close touch with his sources of inspiration, but as long as he has enough money to live in the manner to which he has become accustomed, will he turn out any more major works of the stature of *The Quare Fellow* or *The Hostage*?

In the Theatre Festival of 1961 I presented a new play by a young, self-educated sculptor called James McKenna. This play, *The Scatterin'*, was too 'Irish' to have more than a modest success in Stratford, E.15. However, his writing and that of Tom Murphy and James Douglas as well as various Abbey playwrights, shows so much promise that I personally have no fears for the future of Irish drama. The new Abbey Theatre will be functioning at worst before 1970 and this should give a further impetus to the latent talent of the country in the field of dramatic writing. It is up to Brendan to take his proper place in the ranks of future Irish great playwrights. We can only hope that increasing maturity will give him the diligence which is all that is necessary for him to do so.